FOWLTOWN

Neamathla, Tutalosi Talofa
& the first battle of the Seminole Wars

Dale Cox & Rachael Conrad

2017

ISBN-13: 978-0692977880
ISBN-10: 0692977880

Old Kitchen Books
4523 Oak Grove Road
Bascom, Florida 32423

www.oldkitchen.org

Cast forth lightning, and scatter them:
shoot out thine arrows, and destroy them.
Psalms 144: 6

This book is respectfully dedicated to our friends
Clayton Penhallegon, Dr. Gordon Miller
& Farris Powell (Blue Heron)

Table of Contents

Introduction

The story of Fowltown is in many ways the story of all of the Native Americans of the Southeastern United States. The Tutalosi, as they were called in their own language, were part of the Hitchiti talwa of the Lower Creeks. They were the descendants of an ancient people that many archaeologists believe lived on the Chattahoochee, Flint and Apalachicola Rivers before their arrival of the Mississippians in around 900 A.D. Their own descendants are now part of the Muscogee (Creek) Nation of Oklahoma.

This book is more than a history of a battle, although the Battle of Fowltown was one of the most significant military actions in American history. It is the story of how a courageous chief and his small band of warriors waged a five year war to protect their land, homes and way of life. Neamathla was a Native American patriot, as were the warriors who fought alongside of him. They were treated as renegades and outlaws by the whites of their day, but the passage of 200 years has made it possible for us to tell the story of their courageous stand against a young country that would become the greatest power that the world has ever seen.

We owe a debt of gratitude to many people, organizations and institutions for their assistance in the research and writing of this volume. Our special appreciation is due to Clayton Penhallegon and Dr. Gordon Miller of Decatur County, Georgia. They assisted us with ideas, information and joined us in the field as we searched for traces of the village on Four Mile Creek. We could not have completed this project without their encouragement and assistance. We are also indebted to Dr. Brian Rucker of Pensacola State College, Dr. Joe Knetsch of Tallahassee, Dr. Nancy White of the University of South Florida, Dean DeBolt of the University of West Florida, Gregg Harding of the University of West Florida, Joyce Southard of the University of West Florida, Christopher D. Kimball of the Seminole Wars Foundation, John and Mary Lou Missall of the Seminole Wars Foundation, Mike Bunn of Historic Blakeley State Park, Sue Tindel, Linda Smith of the West Gadsden Historical Society, Savannah Brininstool, Farris Powell (Blue Heron), Heidi Conrad, Pearl Cox, William Cox, Alan Cox and the late "Judge" E.W. Carswell.

Our appreciation must also be extended to the staffs of the following institutions: Florida State Archives, Georgia Archives, Alabama State Archives,

University Archives and West Florida History Center at the University of West Florida, Georgia Historical Society, Bradley Library in Columbus (GA), Willard Library in Evansville (IN), Fort Smith Public Library in Fort Smith (AR), Richland Library in Columbia (SC), the Library of Congress, the National Archives, and the National Archives of Great Britain.

Many others too numerous to name have assisted me in one way or another through the years in the writing of this book. Thank you.

May God bless and keep you.

Dale Cox & Rachael Conrad
October 29, 2017

FOWLTOWN

Neamathla, Tutalosi Talofa
& the first battle of the Seminole Wars

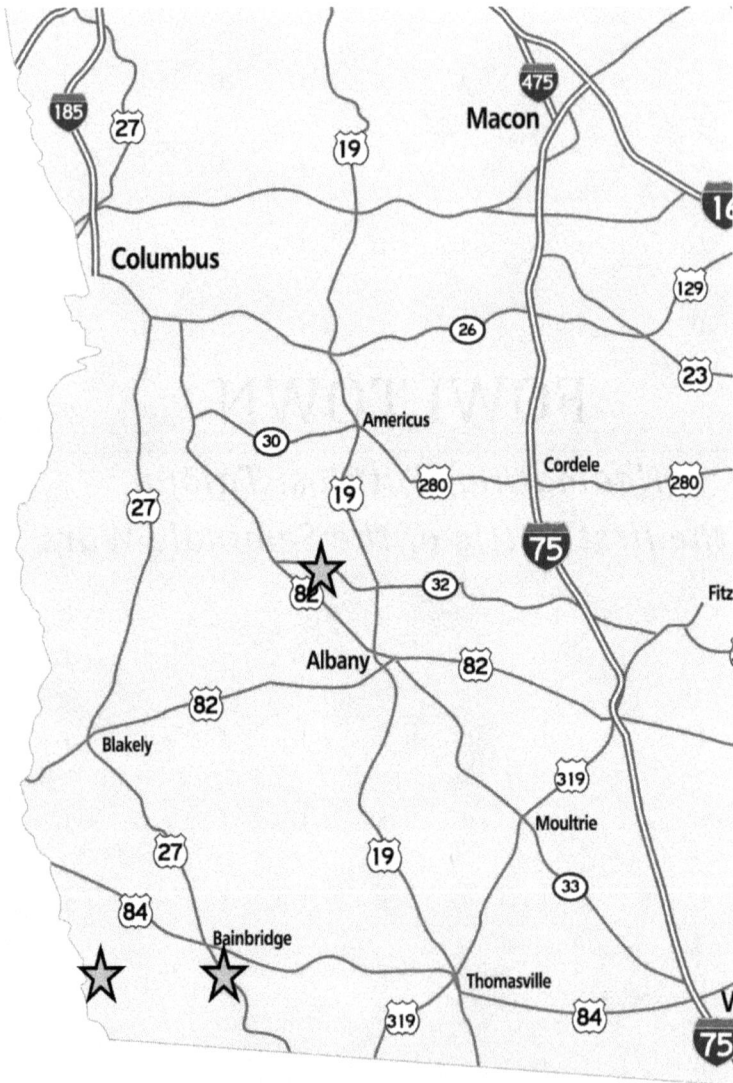

Fowltown Sites in Georgia

1

FOWLTOWN

THE BATTLE OF FOWLTOWN took place in Southwest Georgia on November 21-23, 1817. It was a small encounter as battles go. Casualties were light and neither side achieved real advantage over the other. This skirmish near Four Mile Creek in Decatur County, however, was one of the most significant encounters in American history. Fowltown was the spark that ignited a conflagration that burned on the southern frontier of the United States for more than forty years. Thousands of lives were lost in this war – or series of wars as most historians view it – and one of the country's greatest humanitarian tragedies was its ultimate result.

The name Fowltown is translated from the term Tutalosi Talofa, which in the Hitchiti language means "Chicken Town" or "Fowl Town." It is often described as a Seminole or Miccosukee village but was actually a Lower Creek community. When first described by Col. Benjamin Hawkins in 1799, Tutalosi Talofa was one of four villages that made up the Hitchiti talwa (tribal town). Its residents spoke the common language of the Lower Creeks, a dialect also used by the Miccosukee who then lived in North Florida. Hawkins had been appointed by George Washington as the principal agent to the Creeks and the Superintendent of Indian Affairs for the tribes south of the Ohio River and visited the town during one of his journeys to the Lower Creek country. He wrote that it was located on a branch of Kinchafoonee Creek, a large stream that flows into the Flint River just north of present-day Albany, Georgia:

> Tut-ta-lo-see; (fowl;) on a creek of that name, twenty miles west from Hit-che-too-che. This is a fine creek on a bed of limestone; it is a branch of Kitch-o-foo-ne; the land bordering on the creek, and for eight or nine miles in the direction towards Hit-che-too-che, is leve, rich, and fine for cultivation, with post and black oak, hickory, dogwood and pine. The villagers have good worm fences, appear industrious, and have large stocks of cattle, some hogs and horses; they appear decent and orderly, and are desirous of preserving a friendly intercourse with their neighbors; they have this year, 1799, built a square.[1]

The creek on which the town was located in 1799 is still called Fowltown Creek today. It rises in Terrell County and flows generally to the southeast into Lee County where it merges with the Kinchafoonee. It is spring-fed and runs through an area of impressive limestone outcrops:

> Fowltown Creek has a southeasterly course through the southwest corner of Lee County and empties into Kinchafoonee Creek at Palmyra, 5 miles northwest of Albany. Unlike the latter stream, there is a narrow swamp along Fowltown Creek for its entire course in the county. On both sides of the swamp, however, escarpments rise from 20 to 30 feet above the bottom land. They are highest at the mouth of the creek and get lower as the head is approached. The respective crests, however, are about at the same level and probably belong to the second terrace.[2]

---

[1] Col. Benjamin Hawkins, *Creek Confederacy and a Sketch of the Creek Country*, Savannah, 1848:65.
[2] J.E. Brantley, "A Report on the Limestones and Marls of the Coastal Plain of Georgia," *Bulletin No. 21*, Atlanta: 148.

The site of the town was reported to be about 20 miles west of the Flint River, which would place it near the modern community of Sasser. Tutalosi Talofa was the westernmost of a cluster of Lower Creek villages that had been established in the area by 1799. The others were Aumucculee, the settlements of Jack and William Kinnard, Hitchatoochee ("Little Hitchiti"), Otellewhoyaunau ("Hurricane Town") and some smaller communities of Hitchiti on Chickasawhatchee Creek. Aumuccalee is often called Chehaw because its people were part of the Cheaha who lived in a primary town on the Chattahoochee River. The inhabitants of these villages all spoke the Hitchiti language and were linked by marital and other connections.[3]

The note by Col. Hawkins that the people of Fowltown had built a "square" is important as the traditional square was a focal point of permanent Creek settlements. The village's square would have included four structures, each facing inward and each located on a different side of a central common ground. These buildings included a cabin for the principal chief, which faced east into the common area; the warrior's cabin, which faced south; the cabin of the beloved men, which faced north, and the cabin of the young people and their associates, which faced west. Groups were seated in these structures according to the purposes by which they were named and the square was the place of evening gatherings and important councils for the village.[4]

Benjamin Hawkins, who saw many such village squares, described them in 1799:

> Choo-co-thluc-co, (big house), the town house of public square, consists of four square buildings of one story facing each other, forty by sixteen feet, eight feet pitch; the entrance at each corner. Each building is a wooden frame, supported on posts set in the ground,

---

[3] Hawkins, *Creek Confederacy and a Sketch of the Creek Country*, 1848: 64-65.
[4] *Ibid.*

covered with slabs, open in front like a piazza, divided into three rooms, the back and ends clayed, up to the plates. Each division is divided lengthwise, into two seats; the front, two feet high, extending back half way, covered with reed-mats or slabs; then a rise of one foot, and it extends back, covered in like manner, to the side of the building. On these seats, they lie or sit at pleasure.[5]

Fowltown was among the villages that in 1799-1800 supported the machinations of the famed adventurer and pirate William Augustus Bowles. This tightened their bond with the Miccosukee, who lived on the east side of the lake of that name in Leon County, Florida, and established something of a military alliance between the two communities. It is not clear whether any of the village's warriors took part in Bowles' extended siege and capture of the Spanish fort of San Marcos de Apalache, but it is certainly possible.

Other Lower Creek towns, particularly Coweta and Cusseta, did not support Bowles. This difference of opinion marked the beginning of a more serious division between upper towns of the Lower Creeks, which were clustered around and below today's Columbus, Georgia, and the lower towns, which extended down the Chattahoochee and Flint Rivers to the point where they merged to form the Apalachicola on the border of Spanish Florida. This division became more pronounced over the next two decades and would lead many of the Lower Creeks to join the Seminoles and Miccosukees.

The decision by Fowltown and the neighboring villages to support the "State of Muskogee" scheme also marked the beginning of a major influx of maroons (escaped slaves) into their area. Bowles sought to strengthen his "army" by sending war parties to kidnap slaves from farms and plantations along the Georgia frontier. His "privateer" (i.e. pirate) vessels also took blacks found on captured merchant ships and brought them into Florida via the Apalachicola River. A town populated by these individuals grew on the Flint River under the leadership of

---

[5] *Ibid.*

Philotouche. He and his followers were among the key ancestors of the people identified by many today as the Black Seminoles.

The division that the Bowles intervention created between Tutalosi Talofa and prominent Lower Creek towns such as Cusseta and Coweta simmered for nearly ten years. The interloper was captured and turned over to Spain in 1804 and efforts by his assistance to continue his enterprises failed. Bitterness, however, continued between his former followers and those who had remained loyal to the Big Warrior and Little Prince, the nominal leaders of the Upper and Lower Creeks respectively.

This situation changed dramatically in 1812-1813 with the emergence of a charismatic religious leader among the Creeks. Josiah Francis (Hillis Hadjo) was a metis trader and metal artisan who lived among the Alabama and Coushatta people near the point where the Coosa and Tallapoosa Rivers joined to form the Alabama. He was married to Polly Moniac, the half-sister of the prosperous and well-known Creek businessman Samuel Moniac. Francis was the uncle of David Moniac, the first Native American to graduate from the U.S. Military Academy at West Point, and Polly was a relative of the powerful Creek leader Alexander McGillivray.

The Muscogee (Creek) Confederacy was at the height of its power when Col. Benjamin Hawkins arrived as the representative of the U.S. government. McGillivray had waged a successful predatory war against the white frontiers and President George Washington was forced to bargain with him to bring the conflict to an end. The Treaty of New York, signed in 1790, established peace between the United States and the Creeks, designated a formal boundary separating the two nations, provided for payments or "annuities" to be paid to certain chiefs and included an agreement that whites living in the Creek Nation would be subject to Native American law.[6]

The document also included an agreement that the United States would assist the Creeks in adopting a "plan of civilization." McGillivray supported this idea, which would fundamentally change his nation from a

---

[6] Treaty of New York, 1790.

society of warriors and hunters to a yeoman-like culture of farmers and ranchers. The idea proved very controversial and ultimately led to the rise of Josiah Francis as a prophet and the Creek War of 1813-1814.

Francis became disillusioned by the changes that he saw taking place among his people. Traditional ways were being lost, Col. Hawkins exerted more and more power over the affairs of the Creeks and white settlers pushed against the limits of the nation from the East, West and North. Alcoholism was reaching epidemic proportions and debts owed to white trading firms – particularly John Forbes & Company – were crushing down on the Creeks and forcing them to make large cessions of land to meet their obligations. The Forbes Purchase in Florida, for example, included an estimated 1.2 million acres that were lost to the nation – as well as to the Miccosukee and Seminole – for little more than a balancing of account. Debts owed to the trading companies began to grow again almost as soon as they had been expunged.

The situation was troubling, but Josiah Francis found an answer in the teachings of the Shawnee Prophet. Once a town drunk named Lalawithika ("Noisy Rattle"), the Prophet had fallen into a coma or stupor so deep that his friends and family believed him to be dead and began to prepare for his funeral. At this instant, however, Lalawithika opened his eyes and announced that he had visited the Master of Breath. He had been shown a heaven filled with game and honey that awaited those who lived virtuously and according to their traditional practices. He had also been shown a hell where sinners were subjected to a variety of tortures. The whites, he announced, were the spawn of the great serpent that lived in the sea and the Native Americans were to stop following their ways. They were to return to a life of hunting in the forests and no more land should be given up to the whites without the agreement of all of the tribes. The Shawnee were to unite with other nations to form a defensive line that stretched from the Great Lakes to the Gulf of Mexico. They were to do no harm to anyone, but they were to fight united to save their lands and homes if threatened.[7]

---

[7] For a detailed account of the Lalawithika's conversion, please see R. David

Lalawithika stopped drinking and gave up other vices learned from the whites. He changed his name to Tenskwatawa ("Open Door") and established a ministry that eventually reached virtually every Native American tribe east of the Mississippi River and some of those living to its west. Students of his teachings began to have visions of their own and prophets arose in nation after nation.

Josiah Francis probably heard rumors of Tenskwatawa but he gained factual information when the Prophet's brother, Tecumseh, arrived in the South to spread his message. Tecumseh would later rise to prominence in his own right, but in 1811 he was usually referred to simply as the "brother of the Prophet." He was ordered away by the traditional chiefs of the Choctaw, but the Creek Council invited him to speak at its annual meeting that fall. Delegations from the Lower Creeks were also present for the council at Tuckabatchee that fall. Chiefs and warriors from Fowltown may have been there.

Much has been written about Tecumseh's visit to the Creeks and his speech at Tuckabatchee. Unfortunately, much of what is "accepted" about the Creek Council of 1811 bears little resemblance to what really happened. Many writers, for example, have claimed that the Shawnee urged war with the whites and expressed a desire to drive them into the sea. The real message that Tecumseh delivered, however, was one of peace and not war. He described his brother's visions and urged the Creeks to forge an alliance with other nations and return to their traditional ways:

> ...Tecumseh, in the square of Tuckaubatchee, delivered their talk. They told the Creeks not to do any injury to the Americans; to be in peace and friendship with them; not even to steal a bell from any one of any color. Let the white men on this continent manage their affairs their own way. Let the red people manage their affairs their own way....[8]

Edmunds, *The Shawnee Prophet.*

Col. Hawkins learned the contents of Tecumseh's speech from chiefs who were present. They confessed to having been confused by his claims of conversations with the Master of Breath and told him of their conclusion that he was insane. Other writers of the period would claim that they heard Tecumseh speak, but Hawkins was told by the chiefs that no white man was present to hear the speech. Claims that he urged war, in fact, are extremely questionable as every other written version of a speech given by either Tecumseh or the Prophet himself in 1811 and the preceding years called for peace.

Assertions that Tecumseh predicted the Comet of 1811 are also untrue. The great comet was already visible in the skies over Alabama before he arrived in the Creek Nation. Likewise, claims by some writers that he was so angered by the Big Warrior's refusal to join his "war against the whites" that he threatened to stamp his foot upon his return to his own nation and shake down every house in Tuckabatchee are unlikely as his speech to the Creeks did not include a call for war and was more religious in nature.

The Shawnee's message about his brother's religion may have been confusing to the Big Warrior and other traditional leaders, but a few Creeks understood them very well. Josiah Francis was among these. He spent time with the emissaries from Tenskwatawa, asking them questions and learning as much as he could about the teachings of the Prophet. A lesser prophet named Seekaboo was with the delegation that accompanied Tecumseh to the Creek Nation and he remained behind when the rest of the party returned home. He spent the winter of 1811-1812 talking with Francis and other potential converts and his efforts soon produced results when Josiah Francis gave up the ways of the whites, burned his comfortable home to the ground and slaughtered his livestock where it stood.

---

[8] Benjamin Hawkins to Big Warrior, Little Prince and other Chiefs, June 16, 1814, *American State Papers, Indian Affairs*, Volume 1, p. 845.

Francis announced that he too was experiencing visions and began to preach with the fervor of a new convert. He demonstrated a surprising ability to walk down into a stream or river and remain there for hours on end before emerging to announce that he had been communicating with the water spirits. He established a new village – Holy Ground – on the Alabama River and taught a message that closely mirrored that of the Shawnee Prophet.

The news that a prophet was preaching among the Alabama attracted little attention from Benjamin Hawkins and others. The Creek Council had rejected Tecumseh's message and the agent considered the matter to be closed. As a result, he did not realize the significance of the movement that the Prophet Francis started among the Creeks. By the time that Hawkins comprehended the danger posed to the U.S. "plan of civilization," the population of Holy Ground had grown hundreds of warriors.

The followers of the Prophet became known as Red Sticks or Red Clubs because they raised red war clubs in their towns. An attempt by Hawkins and the Creek Council to punish members of the Red Stick party for an attack against white families on the Duck River by executing the Little Warrior and members of his party backfired when Francis and other Red Stick leaders ordered an attack on Tuckabatchee itself. Civil war exploded among the Creeks and the Big Warrior and his supporters found themselves in a fight for their lives. Had the Red Sticks not run low on ammunition, they might well have cleansed the nation of its white-allied leaders during the summer of 1813.

White and metis militia troops from the Mississippi Territory – which then included parts of Alabama – brought the war down on their own settlements by attempting a preemptive strike on a Red Stick supply party that was returning from Pensacola with ammunition. The Red Sticks, led by Peter McQueen of Tallassee, defeated Col. James Caller's militia troops at the Battle of Burnt Corn Creek on July 27, 1813. Some of the retreating militiamen joined the settlers that had crowded into Fort Mims, a stockade thrown up around the home of Samuel Mims in the

Tensaw settlement. The families of warriors slain at Burnt Corn Creek forced Francis to call off his planned final assault on Tuckabatchee and send the Red Stick army instead against Fort Mims. The stockade fell and over 250 men, women and children were slain on August 30, 1813.

News of the Red Stick victories electrified both the Creek Nation and the white frontier. In Georgia, Fowltown was one of the communities that took notice as messengers arrived to spread news of the Prophet's message and the successes of the Red Stick warriors.

2

NEAMATHLA

FOWLTOWN GREW IN STRENGTH AND SIZE during the 15 years after it was first described by Benjamin Hawkins. The town was already prosperous when visited by the agent in 1799 and this prosperity continued to expand during the years that followed. Unlike the towns on the nearby Flint River, the site of Tutalosi on upper Fowltown Creek was ideal for farming. The valley of the creek was rich and the fields of the village expanded as its inhabitants cleared more and more bottom land of its grown of longleaf pine, hickory, dogwood, oak and other trees. The surrounding pine forests were good for raising free range livestock and the herds of Fowltown grew accordingly. The population, meanwhile, also expanded. Roughly 50 people had lived in the town in 1799 but this number had grown to several hundred by 1813.

The leadership of Fowltown by the beginning of the Creek War had been inherited by Eneah Emathla. The title "eneah emathla" translates literally to "fat next to warrior" in the Hitchiti language. In this case, "fat" did not mean obese or overweight, but that he was large in courage. "Next to warrior" probably referred to the fact that he was not the tustennugee or primary warrior of Hitchiti itself, but instead the war chief of a subsidiary town. The Hitchiti language had no written form so white writers used phonetics to spell their names. Eneah Emathla's was spelled in a variety of ways, with Neamathla being the most common both in his time and today. Other variations included Eneheemathla, Eneheemarthla, Eneheemautby, etc. Because Tutalosi Talofa included no fewer than three leaders named Eneah Emathla, the spelling "Neamathla" will be used here to identify him as the principal chief of the village.[9]

Neamathla was one of the most remarkable Native American leaders of his time. If age estimates given in 1836 are accurate, he was born in the 1750s. The Hitchtiti were then still concentrated on the lower Chattahoochee River and he likely spent his childhood there. Perhaps the most intriguing account of the chief was the second-hand version written by Washington Irving, the famed author of *The Legend of Sleepy Hollow* and other classics of American literature. Irving cultivated a friendship with William P. Duval, the Territorial Governor of Florida in 1822-1834. Duval knew Neamathla well and described him as one of the most remarkable men that he had ever met:

> ...He was a remarkable man; upward of sixty years of age, about six feet high, with a fine eye, and a strongly-marked countenance, over which he possessed great command. His hatred of white men appeared to be mixed with contempt: on the common people he looked down with infinite scorn. He seemed unwilling to acknowledge any superiority of rank or dignity in Governor Duval, claiming to associate with him on terms of equality as two great chieftains.[10]

Duval told Irving that Neamathla could command his warriors with a mere look and that – by the early 1820s at least – his hatred of the whites had no bounds:

---

[9] Spellings given in various original documents; For evidence of three individuals titled Eneah Emathla at Fowltown, please see the treaty executed with the British at Nicolls' Outpost, Florida, on March 10, 1814.

[10] Washington Irving, "Conspiracy of Neamathla" in *The Works of Washington Irving*, Author's Revist Edition, Volume XVI, Woolfer's Roost, New York, G.P. Putnam, 1863, page 297.

...This country belongs to the red man; and if I had the number of warriors at my command that this nation once had, I would not leave a white man on my lands. I would exterminate the whole. I can say this to you, for you can understand me: you are a man; but I would not say it to your people. They'd cry out I was a savage, and would take my life. They cannot appreciate the feelings of a man that loves his country.[11]

The chief's determination to protect his land would characterize his relations with the whites time and again. During one meeting with Gov. Duval, he became quite animated on the topic and made clear that he would fight to the death if need be to preserve the right of his people to live where they chose:

...He held in his hand a long knife, with which he had been rasping tobacco; this he kept flourishing backward and forward, as he talked, by way of giving effect to his words, brandishing it at times within an inch of the governor's throat. He concluded his tirade by repeating, that the country belonged to the red men, and that sooner than give it up, his bones and the bones of his people should bleach upon its soil.[12]

Neamathla was a young man when the lower towns on the Chattahoochee agreed to support the British during the American Revolution. Thomas Perryman, the chief of Tocktoethla, was the son of an English trader and led Lower Creek forces into battle against the rebels in both Georgia and along the Florida frontier north of St. Augustine. When the British later returned to Florida during the War of 1812, Perryman and Neamathla were among the first chiefs to answer their call. This may indicate that the Fowltown chief had taken part in the

---

[11] *Ibid.*, pp. 297-298.
[12] *Ibid.*, pp. 301-302.

border fighting during the American Revolution. Positive proof, however, has not yet been found.[13]

The chiefs of Fowltown told Benjamin Hawkins during his 1799 visit that they were desirous of good relations with their neighbors. Neither they nor he, however, anticipated the sudden return of William Augustus Bowles to the Lower Creek country that year. It is not known if the Tutalosi were among the warriors who joined the adventurer's forces during his siege of the Spanish fort at San Marcos de Apalache (St. Marks), but the Miccosukee were definitely involved and the Hitchiti were closely allied with them. If the Fowltown warriors joined Bowles at any point, Neamathla was undoubtedly at their head.[14]

It was less than ten years after the seizing of William Augustus Bowles during the Creek Council at Tuckabatchee that the Red Stick movement began to rise among the Alabama and Coushatta towns on the Coosa, Tallapoosa and Alabama Rivers. The attack by the whites on the Red Stick supply party at Burnt Corn Creek and the subsequent fall of Fort Mims electrified the borderlands. The Big Warrior and other supporters of Col. Hawkins and the "plan of civilization" found themselves in retreat and the Prophet Francis did his best to capitalize on the situation. He knew that the downstream towns on the Chattahoochee River – along with their subsidiaries on the Flint – were not over the schism that had developed with Coweta, Cusseta and other upriver Lower Creek towns over the presence of Bowles in the Nation. Francis now sought to capitalize on these frosty relations by sending messengers to the lower Chattahoochee.

The Prophet's plan called for the lower towns to join with the Seminoles and form one wing of a two-pronged army that would lay

---

[13] See Edward J. Cashin, *The King's Ranger: Thomas Brown and the American Revolution on the Southern Frontier*, Athens: University of Georgia Press, 1989.
[14] The best modern account of Bowles' second appearance among the Creeks is Gilbert C. Din, *War on the Gulf Coast: The Spanish Fight against William Augustus Bowles*, University Presses of Florida, 2012.

siege to Coweta and break forever the power of Hawkins and the chiefs who supported him:

> Notwithstanding the loss the Prophets have sustained, they express confidence in the successful issue of their plan. Several of their party have lately been down on Chattahoochee, encouraging the Indians, within and without our limits, to join them; and urge an immediate junction of all their forces, for an attack on Coweta, which was determined on by the Prophets, and to take place on Friday next. They are determined, if they can, to destroy Coweta, and Tuckaubatchee in terrorem. After that they should go towards Savannah river, and were determined to give Colonel Hawkins a chace and take him, unless he was on a fleet horse, before he got there.[15]

The teachings of the Prophet struck a chord at Fowltown and with Neamathla in particular. He had seen firsthand the loss of territory experienced by the Creeks due to the Treaty of New York, which had turned over hunting grounds east of the Oconee River to the whites. He had also seen the massive land cession exacted in Florida by the Forbes Purchase. Whatever good feelings the Tutalosi people might have held for their white neighbors in 1799 were rapidly evaporating by 1813. The Red Stick movement appealed to them, especially the call for a Native American alliance that would halt the westward expansion of the United States.

The messengers from Holy Ground also found receptive audiences at the towns of the Miccosukee and the Yuchi. Even the chiefs of the Eufaulas, among whom the Perryman family held positions of leadership, warned Hawkins that they would be forced to join the Red

---

[15] Lower Creek chiefs to Col. Benjamin Hawkins, included in Hawkins to the Secretary of War, September 26, 1813, *American State Papers: Indian Affairs*, Volume I, page 854.

Sticks unless the whites could help them quickly. In a message to Col. Hawkins, they explained the power of the Red Stick message:

> ...[T]hey boasted much, and declared the inability of the white people to fight them in the field, or from their forts; boasted of the immense slaughter they made at Mimms's fort, and quantity of property taken in that expedition; if the red people would unite, nothing could withstand them: and those who would not join, were to be put to death, and this was the last warning they were to have. The chiefs of Eufaulau, having made this discovery, gave notice to Coweta, they could be with them with their warriors, and those of four other towns; and if they could get ammunition, would make common cause with them and their white brethren. They directed that Mr. Cornells should be sent off immediately to Colonel Hawkins, with this information; and added, if our white friends can come soon, the Indians on both sides of our line of limits will join them, and if delayed, they, from their fears, will be compelled to join the Red Clubs.[16]

Events outpaced the ability of the aging U.S. agent to respond. A force of 100 warriors from Miccosukee – the main fighting force of that town – arrived on the Flint where they were joined by Neamathla and the Fowltown warriors. Some of the nearby Cheaha and Osoochee joined as well and the entire party started west for Yuchi on the Chattahoochee River. From there they planned to join the planned Red Stick attack on Coweta.

The forces loyal to the Big Warrior, however, had scouts out and they were able to capture an advance party from this new force of Red Sticks. The information learned from these prisoners was so alarming that the Big Warrior, Little Prince and the chiefs who supported them

---

[16] *Ibid.*

raised a force of warriors from five towns and ordered a preemptive strike down the Chattahoochee:

> The head quarters of the friendly Indians are still at Coweta. We have some Seminoles, of Miccasooky, near St. Marks; about one hundred have crossed Chattahoochee, and been joined by some Uchees and Creeks of Tuttallosee. They gave out they were on the way to join the Prophet's party, for a combined attack on Coweta, and then the white people; the friendly Indians have sent a strong party from five towns to meet them. It is probable they met yesterday; and if their object is as stated, they will be attacked.[17]

The result was the Battle of Uchee Creek, so named because it took place at the primary Yuchi town on the lower reaches of Uchee Creek in today's Russell County, Alabama. The Red Stick force – which included Neamathla and the Fowltown warriors – was surprised and defeated:

> The friendly Indians attacked the Uchees, killed three of them, destroyed all their houses and provisions, with the loss of two horses killed and two wounded. The Seminoles retreated back towards Miccasooky, near St. Mark's. The war party were concentrating their force at Tuckaubatchee, to move on eastwardly, and against the friendly Indians at Coweta. We are nearly one thousand strong there. Terms of peace have been offered Coweta: "Give up four chiefs who are named, and join us against the white people, and we are friends." Peace with them, on any terms, is refused, unless under authority from the President.[18]

---

[17] Col. Benjamin Hawkins to the Secretary of War, October 11, 1813, *American State Papers – Indian Affairs*, Volume I, pp. 853-854.
[18] Col. Benjamin Hawkins to the Secretary of War, October 18, 1813, *American*

The Big Warrior's forces in the battle were led by William McIntosh, the war chief of Coweta and a first cousin of U.S. Rep. George Troup of Georgia. McIntosh was the son of Capt. William McIntosh and his Creek wife. His mother's people called him Tustenuggee Hutke or "White Warrior." He had led the execution squads sent out to execute Little Warrior and other followers of the Prophet Francis and by the fall of 1813 was in primary command of the defense of the Hawkins-allied chiefs who had gathered at Coweta. He would emerge from the Creek War of 1813-1814 as a hated enemy of the Red Sticks and Seminoles.

His destruction of the Yuchi town was a severe blow and warning to the downriver groups that were showing interest in joining the Red Stick movement. It was also unexpected. Neamathla and the other chiefs gathered on Uchee Creek had not been expecting a preemptive strike. The blow sent them reeling.

Col. Hawkins noted in his report that the Miccosukee warriors retreated back to Florida following the battle. He did not immediately mention, however, that they were joined by hundreds of Tutalosi, Osoochee, Yuchi and others. The Battle of Uchee Creek was fought more than 50 miles from Fowltown but it spelled the end of the prosperous town on Fowltown Creek. Neamathla led his people down the Flint as part of a mass evacuation of the Lower Creek towns that had taken part in the battle. These groups soon concentrated again near the confluence of the Chattahoochee and Flint Rivers on the border of Spanish Florida.

The Tutalosi were hastened in their flight by a harsh warning from Benjamin Hawkins:

> I have ordered the Indians to take sides; all who are
> not for the chiefs are hostile, and will be treated
> accordingly. There is to be no neutrals; the evidence

State Papers – Indian Affairs, Volume I, page 857.

required of their having joined the chiefs is to give battle to the adherents of the Prophets.[19]

Hawkins later denied any role in forcing the evacuation of the Fowltown people from the prosperous townsite that they had occupied since before 1799. "They have left us," he wrote, "we did not drive them away." For Neamathla and his followers, however, there could be no mistaking the agent's words. Unwilling to join the forces of the Big Warrior in battle against the Red Sticks, they chose to leave rather than face attack.[20]

---

[19] *Ibid.*
[20] Col. Benjamin Hawkins to the Big Warrior, Little Prince and other Creek Chiefs, June 16, 1814.

3

THE BRITISH

U.S. AUTHORITIES believed that the Creek War was instigated by the British as a means of opening a new front in the War of 1812. Tecumseh, they said, had been sent to the Creeks by British agents from Canada who had offered arms, supplies and even money for scalps. Some historians continue to repeat these claims as fact today even though they were completely untrue. Tecumseh's visit to the Creeks was in 1811, well before the start of the War of 1812. There were no British agents at Prophet's Town (Tippecanoe) in Indiana when he left for Alabama. He traveled at the behest of his brother, Tenskwatawa, and carried a message of peace and unity, not a call for war. The War of 1812, in fact, was initiated by the United States and not Great Britain.

The first request from the Creeks for support from Great Britain went out only a few weeks before the Battle of Uchee Creek and it was from Thomas Perryman and other chiefs from the lower Chattahoochee River, not the Prophet Francis. News of the militia attack on Peter McQueen's party at Burnt Corn Creek had alarmed the towns not yet involved in the civil war already raging between the Red Sticks and the "Big Warrior party." Realizing that the battle would cause the war to expand, Perryman feared that white armies would invade Creek country and would likely not differentiate between peaceful and non-peaceful towns. He knew that the warriors of the towns on the lower Chattahoochee would need arms and ammunition to defend themselves if attacked by the whites so he led a delegation of chiefs to Pensacola in search of munitions. Included in the party were William Perryman (son of Thomas), Alexander Durant and others. They reached the Spanish capital just as a ship flying the Union Jack arrived in the harbor.

The vessel was the HMS *Herald,* a 20-gun British warship that had been cruising the Gulf of Mexico in search of U.S. prey. She had taken the merchant ship *Adeline Cecilia* on August 13, 1813, sending her back to Nassau in the Bahamas as a prize. The *Herald* continued her cruise, arriving off Pensacola during the second week of September 1813.[21]

The sight of the warship was a welcome one to Thomas and William Perryman, Durant and the others. They quickly made contact with Lt. Edward Hanfield, who agreed to come ashore to meet with them. The chiefs met with the British lieutenant on September 11, 1813, handing him a crudely written plea for military support:

> We hope you will eade and assist us as your alis and friends Sir you know that our four fathers owned the Lan Where we now live But and Ever since our father the King of Grate Briton Left us the Americans had Ben Robing us of our Rights and now the americans has maid war against our nations and we aply for armes and amenisun to defend our silves from so Greid a Enemy and as you Know that this nations all ways was frinds to the English we hope you will send us Seplys by Henry Durgen as soon as possible and we hope that you will send sum of our old frind the British troops to eade and assist us a ganst our Enemeys.[22]

The request was probably written by Henry Durgen, a trader who had been living at Opithlucco among the Upper Creeks when Benjamin Hawkins first arrived as U.S. agent during the 1790s. He was in Pensacola when the chiefs arrived and agreed to represent them in the

---

[21] *The London Gazette,* June 18, 1814, Issue 16909, Page 1256.
[22] Thomas Perryman, Capt. William Perryman, Alexander Durant and Noah Hoeo to the Governor of New Providence, National Archives of Great Britain.

Bahamas. The phonetical spellings and strained grammar of the letter should likely be attributed to him and not to the chiefs. Whether Durgen had recently fled the Upper Creek towns due to the war or had relocated to Florida some time before is not known.[23]

The *Herald* reached Nassau on October 28, 1813. Durgen was introduced to Gov. Cameron who quickly recognized that the plea for help from the chiefs offered an important opportunity for Great Britain to open a new front in the War of 1812. If the Creek and Seminole warriors could be supplied and enlisted in the war effort, they would form a powerful auxiliary force capable of assisting in any major British invasion of the Gulf Coast. Cameron wasted no time and penned a letter that same day to Earl Bathurst, the Secretary of State for War and Colonies. He urged that the Native Americans be supplied with the arms and ammunition that they sought.[24]

Bathurst replied on January 21, 1814, with news that he was authorizing the Royal Navy to support and arm the Indians on the Florida coast. The move was part of a plan to open a Gulf Coast campaign against the United States. Royal Marines would be sent to Spanish Florida where they would organize, supply, arm and train Creek and Seminole warriors. A battalion of Colonial Marines would also be raised there by enlisting maroons (escaped slaves) and free blacks into the service of the crown. This force could then support a British operation against Mobile Bay. If Mobile could be taken, it would be used as a base for a land campaign across the Mississippi and Louisiana Territories to the Mississippi River north of New Orleans. The vital Crescent City would be cut off from river commerce and might even fall without the firing of a shot.

Planning such operations takes time and formal orders were not handed down to the Royal Navy until March 30, 1814. The British had no way of knowing it, but the Red Sticks had suffered a devastating defeat just three days earlier at the Battle of Horseshoe Bend.

---

[23] Benjamin Hawkins, *Letters of Benjamin Hawkins*, page 169.
[24] Gov. Charles Cameron to Earl Bathurst, October 28, 1813, National Archives of Great Britain.

The location to which the Fowltown people had gone during the winter of 1813-1814 is not known, but by the spring they were in the vicinity of Thomas Perryman's town on the lower Chattahoochee River. This long-settled and prosperous community was called Tocktoethla ("River Junction") and lay along the east side of the river in what is now Seminole County, Georgia. Archaeologists excavated a small section of the town during the 1940s and 1950s as part of their work at the well-known Fairchild's Landing site. The completion of Lake Seminole in 1958 inundated much of the site but a section of the old bluff still projects above the surface of the reservoir. The surrounding fields and home sites likely extended into the limits of today's Fairchild Park.[25]

A map prepared by Capt. George Woodbine of the Royal Marines during the summer of 1814 has been found in the National Archives of Great Britain. It shows symbols for a scattered settlement on the opposite side of the Chattahoochee from Perryman's town in what is now Jackson County, Florida. The label "Fowl Town" appears there. This indicates that at least by the late spring of 1814, Neamathla had settled his people on the bluff across from Thomas Perryman. The Woodbine map also shows a settlement of Yuchis living nearby along with groups labeled "Oaketee Ockanee" (Okitiyakani) and "Saackulo Tribe" (Sawokli). All of these had been part of the Red Stick force engaged by the Coweta warriors at the Battle of Uchee Creek.[26]

Archaeologists discovered the site of a Creek settlement at approximately the location shown by the Woodbine map while conducting the Lake Seminole Archeological Survey in 1979-1980. The discovery was confusing at the time because while the site later became part of a reserve established for Econchattimico ("Red Ground King"), that chief's town was known to be located three miles to the south. It now seems likely that the scattered sherds of Creek pottery were the remnants of the short-lived Fowltown that lay west of the Chattahoochee River in Jackson County, Florida.[27]

---

[25] Woodbine Map of 1814, National Archives of Great Britain;
[26] Woodbine Map of 1814.

The refugees from Fowltown, Yuchi, Okitiyakani and Sawokli were the first drops of a coming tidal wave. Maj. Gen. Andrew Jackson's victory over Menawa's warriors at Horseshoe Bend broke the back of the Red Stick movement on the Tallapoosa, Coosa and Alabama Rivers. The Prophet Francis, Peter McQueen and other leaders led their starving people south down the Conecuh and Choctawhatchee Rivers to Spanish Florida. It was the disastrous first chapter in a Trail of Tears for the Muscogee (Creek) people that would not end until virtually the entire nation was forced to make the long journey west to Oklahoma. The next 25 years represented a time of enormous suffering for the Muscogee.

The humanitarian disaster that struck the borderlands of Spanish West Florida in 1814 is little-known and often overlooked. Its magnitude, however, was greater than anything comprehensible today. The suffering men, women and children arrived in the thousands, having lost everything they owned or had ever known:

> ...[S]uch objects I never saw the like of, absolute skin and bone, but cheerfull and resolved to do their utmost against the common enemy. An old man told me, when I asked him how far it was to where the enemy were, and if he knew the way to lead me to them, he said it was seven days Journey to them, (about 300 miles) that he could not miss the way, for it was marked by the graves of his five children.[28]

No estimates were ever made of the number of people who died on the overland journey from the Upper Creek homeland and it is impossible to assemble one today. Thomas Perryman reported - along with Cappachimico, the leader of the powerful Miccosukee - that so many refugees

---

[27] Nancy Marie White, "Archeology at Lake Seminole," Cleveland Museum of Natural History, 1980.
[28] Lt. Col. Edward Nicolls to Admiral Alexander Cochrane, August 12, 1814 – November 1814, Cochrane Papers (Passage probably written on August 12, 1814)

were arriving that they "had created a famine, and were actually eating the corn before it was ripe." The people of Fowltown were among those referred to by the chiefs.[29]

The number of Red Sticks in the swamps of the Escambia, Conecuh and Choctawhatchee Rivers was estimated at from 1,500-3,000 people. 700-1,000 of were warriors. All were desperate for food and supplies. To make matters worse, they were pursued by detachments of mounted white, Creek and Choctaw troops Eyewitness accounts from both north and south of the international border indicate that some of the most aggressive of these mounted parties were led by William Weatherford, the former Red Stick warrior who is often credited with leading the attack on Fort Mims. He surrendered after Horseshoe Bend and became a scout for the U.S. Army. The Spanish in Florida simply could not provide enough food to save the lives of the starving men, women and children. Neither could the Seminole and Miccosukee towns between the Apalachicola and Suwannee Rivers. Their winter supplies were gone and the new year's crop of corn was far from being ready to eat. Rumors spread through the white settlements of Georgia, Tennessee and the Mississippi Territory that that the refugees would soon have no choice but to surrender. Andrew Jackson made clear that Josiah Francis and Peter McQueen would pay for their roles in the war with their lives. Benjamin Hawkins had likewise warned the towns on the lower Chattahoochee and Flint Rivers that they would be treated as enemies if they did not actively join the fight against the Red Sticks.

The outlook was dramatically changed in late May 1814 when the sails of two British warships appeared on the horizon off Apalachicola Bay. The supplies and help requested by Thomas Perryman and the other chiefs at Pensacola the previous year had arrived.

The ships were the HMS *Orpheus* and HMS *Shelburne*. They dropped anchor off Apalachicola Bay on May 10, 1814. On board were 2,000 muskets, ammunition, blankets and other supplies intended for the Creeks and Seminoles. In command of the land force was Brevet 2nd Lt. George Woodbine of the Royal Marines. A former Bahamian merchant and militia officer, he had experience running an illicit trade with the Seminole and Miccosukee towns in Florida.

---

[29] *Ibid.*

Neither the *Orpheus* nor the smaller *Shelburne* could make it into the bay because the channel between St George and St. Vincent Islands was too shallow. Supplies would have to be offloaded on one of the barrier islands and then carried inland in smaller vessels. Capt. Hugh Pigot of the *Orpheus* ordered Woodbine to invite Native American groups in the region to come down and be armed:

> You are hereby directed to proceed up the river Appalachicola and endeavour by every means in your power to procure an interview with the Chiefs of the Creek Nation. You will inform them that the Orpheus Frigate has arrived on the coast with two thousand muskets, ammunition, &c. &c. for them, and...and should cavalry be able to act inform me what arms and furniture they stand in need of.[30]

Woodbine carried out his mission with impressive success. The first chiefs and warriors came aboard the *Orpheus* on May 20, 1814, just ten days after the vessel first dropped anchor off West Pass. Thomas Perryman and Cappachimico arrived soon after. Neamathla and other chiefs were with them. The approved the deposit of both supplies and soldiers on the east end of St. Vincent Island, where huts were built for the reception of both. Sgt. Smith and Corp. Denney of the Royal Marines volunteered to train warriors in light infantry tactics and Capt. Pigot approved:

> It being for the good of His Majesty's Service, I feel it my duty to accept the voluntary offer of your services to instruct the Creek Nations in the use of small arms & assist them against our common enemy the Americans.
>
> For which, it is my positive directions you put yourselves under the command of Brevet Captain Woodbine of the Royal Marines, and follow such orders

---

[30] Capt. Hugh Pigot to Capt. George Woodbine, May 10, 1814, Cochrane Papers.

as he may give from time to time for the performance of this service.

Given under my hand on board
the said ship the 21st May 1814.[31]

Smith and Denney landed on St. Vincent but it is unclear whether any training actually took place there. Woodbine had identified Prospect Bluff, about twenty miles upstream from the bay, as a promising location for the planned British logistical base. The British would then advance to the confluence of the Chattahoochee and Flint Rivers where they would establish a base for operations against American forces in Georgia and the Creek Nation.[32]

The next step in this operation came on May 25 when Woodbine shifted his operations to Prospect Bluff. A large group of Red Sticks, Seminoles and Miccosukees had gathered there and the British officer met in council with them on the same day. Neamathla and several of the other Fowltown chiefs were present:

> ...The Proclamation of the Commander in Chief, I intend to forward in a day or two to Georgia, Tennessee & New Orleans by trusty Indians, who have been appointed at a general meeting of the chiefs, for such purposes, and I have no doubt of several hundred American slaves joining our standard the moment it is raised, which shall be done when the arms are all up, and an encampment formed on the Forks of the River. At this same meeting the chiefs have unanimously decided that all power to conduct operations shall be taken out of their hands and lodged solely in mine, as chief of all, as

---

[31] Hugh Pigot to Sgt. Smith & Corp. Denny, May 21, 1814, Cochrane Papers (Signed aboard HMS Orpheus off the Apalachicola River).
[32] Bvt. Capt. George Woodbine to Capt. Hugh Pigot, May 25, 1814 (I) (not sent), Cochrane Papers.

also the appointment of all officers, and that no interference of a single individual shall be allowed.[33]

Woodbine "accepted" the command on the condition that "they will make prisoners (and give them up to me for the purpose of working on any public works I may order) that they put to death no one but those resisting with arms in their hands." The chiefs agreed to this condition. Thomas Perryman and Cappachimico were appointed as "generals" by the captain who promised to share all reports and intelligence with them and to confer with them on all important subjects. He noted, however, that he knew he could "twist round my finger and induce them to think as I do."[34]

Woodbine knew by this time that the U.S. Army had achieved a bloody victory over the Red Sticks at Horseshoe Bend. He sent the Seminole chief Yellow Hair - who he called the "Young Chief Yellow Hair" - west to Pensacola to bring the refugees in that vicinity to the Apalachicola for arms and ammunition. Yellow Hair lived at the Tamathli town on the west side of the river just below the junction of the Chattahoochee and Flint Rivers.[35]

The British did not hesitate to initiate aggressive action against the United States from their new base on the Apalachicola. Woodbine informed Capt. Pigot on May 28th that he was making efforts to capture an American "spy" reported to be visiting Lower Creek towns further upriver:

> ...I have dispatched a party under the Young Warrior that was on board to seize Wilson the American Spy (who I hear is purchasing cattle up the Country) and also his property, and bring him down here: Should I succeed in catching him I will send him down to you, if you

---

[33] *Ibid.*
[34] *Ibid.*
[35] *Ibid.*

should not have sailed, immediately on the return of the Young Chief Yellow Hair from Pensacola. I purpose sending him to the Big Warrior, and doubt not and doubt not succeeding in gaining every Indian over from the Americans.[36]

Of greater concern to the captain and his officers, however, was the shortage of provisions at Prospect Bluff and the necessity of sending supplies to the Pensacola area so the refugees there could survive the trip to the Apalachicola. The British had not anticipated a need to feed thousands of Red Stick men, women and children. The Forbes & Company store had a cattle herd and was willing to sell beef to meet the military's needs – but at a price:

> I sadly fear that for a few weeks a considerable sum must be spent in purchasing provisions (dry cattle) particularly when the Pensacola party and Negroes come on, they having no land or provisions to maintain themselves until we levy supplies on the states. If a small quantity of goods were sent down here immediately from Providence, I would purchase cattle for government at one half cheaper than getting them from the House here. *I shall be much obliged to you Sir, for particular instructions how I am to act in respect of drawing for the payment of the Cattle sent on to Pensacola, and also for the flour, should it have been delivered, or for any thing else that the present service should absolutely require.*[37]

The thought that expenses for purchasing additional food would continue for "a few weeks" was overly optimistic in the extreme. The British would experience problems in feeding their allies for the duration

---

[36] *Ibid.*
[37] *Ibid.*

of their occupation of Prospect Bluff. Such issues aside, Sgt. Smith and Corp. Denney began their assignment of drilling Native American warriors – including many from Fowltown. Woodbine reported that the young men in particular "appear anxious to learn their exercise, and I have great hopes of our doing some thing very shortly." The training included the use of the muskets brought by the British as well as in bayonet tactics.[38]

A noteworthy council of officers, chiefs and leading warriors was convened on May 28, 1817. Woodbine urged Perryman, Cappachimico, Neamathla and others to be humane in their treatment of prisoners:

> Your father King George sends me among you, to bring arms and ammunition to defend yourselves. Your father got only one letter from you, and I now give you the Answer – Hear – Your father told me to tell you that he had never forgot good children the Creeks, but that many Nations of Enemies had tried for some years past to destroy your Father, but the Great Spirit had stood his friend and had made him so strong that he had beat them all. Your father told me to tell you that he was sorry to hear that those wicked people the Americans, were robbing his children the Creeks of their lands and were driving them, their women & children into the woods like Tigers. Your Father wishes you to talk the straight talk with his Captain about all your business.
>
> Your Father wishes to know what things you want to make you all happy. If you tell me, I will write to his Admiral and Great Warrior, who will send them. Your Father told me to tell you, that he wants to protect all the Indians and to make them into one family that they may unite and drive the Children of the Bad Spirit (the Americans) out of the lands and hunting ground.

---

[38] *Ibid.*

Your father told me to tell you that he wants some Americans, men women & children, and if you will take them all prisoners, instead of killing them, he will send you good presents every year and plenty of Powder & Ball to hunt with.

You must bring them all to me his Captain, and I will write to the Admiral and great Warrior, who will then write to the King your father, all good talks about you.[39]

The request reflects a strong awareness on the part of the British that frontier warfare often degenerated into a bloodfest that was counter to the practices of "civilized" warfare. Woodbine was careful not to place blame on either the Red Sticks or the Americans for such conduct, but he made clear that Great Britain would not countenance the killing and mutilation of prisoners. The preserved copy of his talk provides a remarkable contradiction to old Southern legend that claims the British offered "$10 a scalp" for the hair of American soldiers and settlers. The Native Americans agreed to abide by the standards of conduct outlined by the British:

In the name of all the chiefs of the Creek Nations, now assembled in arms against the Americans, we promise to spare the lives of all prisoners taken, wither man, woman or child, and to give them to Captain Woodbine of the Royal Mairnes who has informed us that they should be a gratefull present to our Father King George.

For all the Chiefs, we sign by their desire,
Thomas Perryman, King of the Seminoles
Cappachamico, King of the Mickasukis

---

[39] Talk of George Woodbine to Chiefs at Prospect Bluff, May 28, 1814, Enclosure #2 in Woodbine to Lt. Hope, HMS Shelbourne, May 31, 1814, Cochrane Papers.

Witness to Signatures
Wm. Hambly[40]

Couriers were sent upriver to Eufaula and other Lower Creek towns, inviting them down to receive arms and ammunition. It did not take long for rumors of the British arrival to reach Col. Hawkins who warned U.S. authorities that a new front was about to be opened in the War of 1812. He did not know it yet, but the Fowltown warriors would be the tip of the British spear.

---

[40] Thomas Perryman and Cappachimico, Promise, May 28, 1814, Enclosure #1 in Woodbine to Lt. Hope, HMS Shelbourne, May 31, 1814, Cochrane Papers.

Okitiyakani – as well as the Seminoles of Florida - to return to their former homes:

> ...They are one people with us. Let the Chiefs of Tutallossee and Oketeyoconne come also, and treat them kindly. They have left us, we did not drive them away. If they have done no mischief, they have nothing to fear; if they have, they must give up the guilty. And, whether guilty or not, they must be safe in coming to see me and talk with us.[43]

The colonel seems to have forgotten about the attack carried out against these and other groups at the Battle of Uchee Creek in October 1813, as well as his warning at the time that any Lower Creeks who refused to fight the Red Sticks would be treated as enemies. These actions had driven Neamathla and other chiefs from their towns and down to the forks of the Chattahoochee and Flint Rivers and the protection of Thomas Perryman. They were more than willing to accept military help from the British to defend themselves against the attacks they expected to come against them for not joining in the fight against the Red Sticks.

Hawkins need not have worried about the Big Warrior and Little Prince leading their followers to join the British. He was likely in the act of writing his long missive to them as they sent out a courier with intelligence for him about the situation on the Apalachicola River:

> The British offered arms and ammunition to all the red people that came and saw them. There was none of the red people that would receive it but two towns, Tuttaloosa and Oketeyocanneee, all below Perryman's and down to see the English. We have not heard of any receiving any ammunition but those two towns. The

---

[43] *Ibid.*

Tuttoloosa and Oketeyocannee people asked for 200 kegs ammunition for each town. The answer was by the English, they could not spare them that quantity. They said they had a talk for the Cussetau and Cowetaw and said you two towns come ahead of them. And they gave them two towns four kegs of cartridges to each town, containing 100 lbs. in each keg; when the Oketeyocannee people got their ammunition they carried it off some distance. A great squall of thunder & lightning come up, and the lightning struck one of their kegs, burnt a good many of their people very badly, one they expect will die, and one of the kegs blew up. They returned again to the English and told them their misfortune. They give them another keg in the room.[44]

The story of the explosive lightning strike was confirmed by Capt. Woodbine. "The lightning on Sunday night struck near a tree near the magazine and blew up one of the largest casks of powder," he reported to Capt. Pigot of the HMS *Orpheus* on May 31, 1814, "but did no more mischief than severely scalding one man." It was strangely prophetic of the disaster that would take place when a U.S. Navy cannonball struck the magazine two years later on July 27, 1816.[45]

The informant who witnessed the warriors of Fowltown and Okitiyakani receiving 800 pounds of cartridges from the British also described the talk that they were given by an officer who warned them against prematurely attacking the Americans:

---

[44] Tustunnuggee Thlucco, Tustunnuggee Hopoi and John Steddam to Benjamin Hawkins, June 13, 1814, Hargrett Rare Book and Manuscript Library, The University of Georgia Libraries, Telamon Cuyler, box 77, folder 33, document 23.

[45] Bvt. Capt. George Woodbine to Capt. Hugh Pigot, May 31, 1814, Cochrane Papers.

You Red people, our Children, We thought you were all done over; and the Heads of our Nation sent us here to see you. We were told you, our Children, were very poor. When we arrived we found it was true, and we make a present to you of this ammunition, not to do any mischief with it, we give it to you for your hunting and support your families. You are not to do any mischief to no person. Whatever you do, do not lift up your hands against the American people. If you do, your nation will be ruined and destroyed.

We understand your nation was fighting one another, which was a bad policy among you. You must quit that if you do not stop it, you will lose the whole of your country. Our Heads gave us a talk which brought us here. We were sent here to Talk to the Cussetau and Cowetaw, these two fires, and also Cherokees, Chickasaw & Choctaw to the whole of the Four Nations, there is none left out. We was sent to come a shore here. A part of our troops is to land near Savannah and Amelia Island, and others are to land below Mobile, which last place will not be for some time. The white people are fighting their own battles, and we are in hopes to have peace with the American people sometime this year. We want the Red people to have no hand in it, in our warfare. We don't want the red people to assist the white people in any of the white peoples' affairs. We do not give you arms and ammunition for that purpose.[46]

Woodbine definitely did not want Fowltown or Okitiyakani to do anything that might bring down the power of the U.S. military on him before the British were ready, but there is some question about the accuracy of the last part of the quoted warning. Perhaps he was warned

---

[46] "Talk of British Officer," incorporated in Tustunnuggee Thlucco, Tustunnuggee Hopoi and John Steddam to Benjamin Hawkins, June 13, 1814.

by chiefs who knew them that spies were present and altered his talk for their benefit. The British absolutely expected the warriors to join them in fighting against the United States and were already providing them with training in light infantry tactics.

Support for the idea that Woodbine was performing a bit of psychological warfare against the United States can be found in a separate talk that the spies – who were boatmen employed by John Stidham – received from Cappachimico of Miccosukee. He asked that it be delivered to the chiefs of Coweta and Cusseta:

> The British give us a fine talk, I have listen to it. I do not like their talk. As soon as the British saw me, they want to give me arms and ammunition. I told them no, I want no such articles among my people, and took nothing from them. They called us their Children; if they offered us some Clothing to hide our nakedness, I should have received it with pleasure but such as arms & ammunition I have an opinion of it – I don't like it – I am sensible of their talk, I understand their ways very well. They sent us a Bowles here once, he acted in the same manner. He was very near bringing our nation into ruin. It will not be long before the British give us a bad talk. Whenever the Cussetau takes this talk I will take it too, but not before. I shall always abide what the Cussetau and Cowetaw do.[47]

Cappachimico by this time had already agreed to support the British war effort, had signed a document agreeing to turn all prisoners over to Capt. Woodbine and was arming his warriors from the magazine at Prospect Bluff despite his claim in the talk that he would not do so. The message was clearly false and the chief knew it. There can be no other real conclusion than that he was intending to deceive or confuse the

---

[47] "Talk of Cappachimico," incorporated in Tustunnuggee Thlucco, Tustunnuggee Hopoi and John Steddam to Benjamin Hawkins, June 13, 1814.

chiefs at Coweta and Cusseta. Col. Hawkins was likely also a target of the fake messages. Cappachimico's mention of Bowles was likely an appeal to the agent's vanity, as he often mentioned the adventurer in his talks and letters to Creek leaders.

The talks carried back up the Chattahoochee definitely confused the U.S.-allied chiefs. They were very suspicious of Fowltown and Okitiyakani and concerned that things were not as promised. They were also wary of a request from the Miccosukee chief that they come down to meet him at Eufaula:

> We are here, and we hear this talk. His talk put us all to a stand, and don't know what to think of it. Those two towns are always sending good talks down this river. We do not know what we shall do with these Lower Towns. We are afraid it will commence in the same manner with the Seminoles as it did with the Upper Towns. There were two places appointed to hold public Talk, one place is broken up by the hostiles. Cowetaus still remains. This place was appointed by you Colo. Hawkins for to hold public talk. We shall send them word for all their Chiefs and Head men to attend the talks at Cowetaw. We are here & don't know what they are doing down there. When they all come here at Cowetau we shall then know what they are doing.[48]

A very different account was also making its way to Hawkins from Christian Limbaugh and Alexander Cornells. The two associates of the agent were on the Chattahoochee River where they learned from Fallausau Hadjo, the chief of Eufaula, and the Wolf Warrior that the British had landed at Apalachicola and were supplying the Seminoles with arms and ammunition. Each town was being given "four large casks

---

[48] Tustunnuggee Thlucco, Tustunnuggee Hopoi and John Steddam to Benjamin Hawkins, June 13, 1814.

of powder and some short muskets in slings and other things." The British officer – undoubtedly Woodbine – gave a very different talk than the one reported by Stidham's employees:

> The red people who had been driven from Tallapoosa must assemble and were assembling between the bay of Pensacola and apalatchicola. They had halted at yellow water and would concentrate their force at Choctau hatche and remain ready for further orders. The plan of the British was to take Mobile, perdido, yellow Water, Choctau hatche, an island near St. Marys, an Island near Savannah and that town and an island near Charleston at the same time. One of his vessels was to set sail immediately for supplies for the Red people and he expected in 25 days to receive the supplies and the time when this plan was to take affect. In the mean time the Indians could be recruiting their strength exhausted by their recent war and famine, and be ready to cooperate with their friends the British who would strike at and occupy all these places at the same time.[49]

This version of the talk clearly indicates that the Native Americans were being armed and supplied ahead of expected combat operations of the United States. The talk also made clear that the warriors would cooperate in the campaign, much the opposite of the one given in the presence of John Stidham's boatmen.

The informants further reported that the Prophet Francis had arrived at Prospect Bluff, as had Tustenuggee Hadjo:

---

[49] Benjamin Hawkins, Report of supplies to the Indians by the British and Spaniards at Pensacola and mouth of Chattahochie, June 14, 1814, Telamon Cuyler Collection, Hargrett Rare Book and Manuscript Library, The University of Georgia Libraries, Box 76, Folder 25, Document 06.

The prophet observed to the Semenolies in presence of the reporters "we have brought our difficulties on ourselves without advise from any one. The old chiefs need not expect we will be given up. We have lost our country and retreated to the sea side where we will fight until we are all destroyed, we are collected and find a few more than 1000 warriors left; and mean to form our settlement on Choctau hatche."

Tustunnuggee Haujo who fled with the fowltown and Oketeyoanne people below the confluence of the Flint & Chattahooches sent a message to the Big Warrior & Little Prince "I have now friends and arms, you compelled me to fly and if you attempt to track me up I shall spill your blood."[50]

The people of Fowltown had survived the aftermath of Uchee Creek and, like Tustennuggee Hadjo, now had friends and arms and were ready to spill the blood of their enemies. Even as Thomas Perryman appeared at Coweta for a council and promised that there was nothing to fear from his direction, Sgt. Smith and Corp. Denney of the Royal Marines traveled up the Apalachicola River to his town. Stocks of arms and ammunition were warehoused there and the two noncommissioned officers resumed their work of instructing warriors in light infantry tactics, including the use of the bayonet. Neamathla had been one of the first chiefs to accept military aid from the British and since he and his people now lived directly across the Chattahoochee River from Perryman's town, there is little doubt that the Fowltown warriors took park in these drills. They were likely joined by the men of the neighboring Okitiyakani, Yuchi, Tamathli and Tellmochesses towns.[51]

---

[50] *Ibid.*

[51] Brig. Gen. J. Graham to Gov. William Hawkins (North Carolina), July 16, 1814, published in the *Daily National Intelligencer*, August 10, 1814; Capt. George Woodbine, Orders to Lt. Smith of July 21, 1814, Cochrane Papers.

Woodbine was so pleased with the efforts of Sgt. Smith that he gave him a field promotion to lieutenant on July 20, 1814. Not only was Smith then "up the Country drilling," but he secured intelligence that Fort Hawkins was not prepared for an attack and that Col. Hawkins and his family were there. He requested that he be allowed to move against the fort and Woodbine agreed. Fowltown and the surrounding communities would take part in the raid:

> The enterprize you have solicited my permission to undertake, I have from your representation of the practicability thereof consented to your attempted. But recollect to temper that laudable ambition you have to distinguish yourself in some dashing affair with prudence, and use every endeavour to obtain correct information of the strength of the object of attack. Should you succeed, I know I need scarcely inform you that "Humanity is the first quality in a truly brave man." The Indians will spare as few as possible but impress it on the minds of the party that accompany you that prisoners are my object, and that I set my face against putting any one not resisting to death or scalping them, and that according to the humanity they shew, so will you report their conduct to me and procure them rewards accordingly. Should any females (of which I understand the Colonels family are likely to be part) fall into your hand, you too well know the duty of an Englishman and a soldier to require my saying a word to you on the line of conduct to pursue.[52]

What might have happened had Smith moved against Fort Hawkins with the full strength of Fowltown and the other villages clustered around Perryman's will never be known. The orders for the attack stood less than 24-hours before Woodbine countermanded them and ordered

---

[52] Capt. George Woodbine, Orders to Lt. Smith of July 21, 1814.

the lieutenant to march instead for Pensacola. News had arrived at Prospect Bluff explaining the magnitude of the humanitarian disaster taking place in the refugee camps along the Conecuh, Escambia and Choctawhatchee Rivers. This alarming intelligence was coupled with word of a possible vulnerability at the American forts above Mobile. A detachment was left to protect the bluff and continue the distribution of arms and ammunition. Capt. Woodbine, meanwhile, headed for Pensacola by ship while Smith and Denney were to move by land at the head of a force of 300 Creek, Seminole and Miccosukee warriors.[53]

British attention now shifted to Pensacola where the Spanish governor was so concerned about rumors of an American attack that he allowed Woodbine to occupy Fort St. Michael – formerly Fort George – which overlooked the town. The captain's commanding officer, Maj. Edward Nicolls of the Royal Marines, arrived at Prospect Bluff a short time later and then followed on to Pensacola. The British and their Red Stick allies at Fort Bowyer at the entrance to Mobile Bay on September 11-12, 1814, an action that ended in disastrous failure for them. The main body then returned to Pensacola to continue recruiting, equipping and training Native American auxiliaries and a battalion of Colonial Marines. It remained there until November 7 when the city was taken by the U.S. army under Maj. Gen. Andrew Jackson. The British then withdrew back to the Apalachicola River where they resumed their original plan of advancing up to the forks of the Chattahoochee and Flint, building a second fort and then launching attacks on the Georgia frontier.[54]

Neamathla and the warriors of Fowltown were not idle during this shift of British activity. Whether by order from Woodbine and Smith or on their own initiative, they moved almost immediately to harass the whites living along near Milledgeville and Fort Hawkins. The first warning of this came from Timothy Barnard, a white trader of long standing who lived on the Flint River with his Yuchi family. He wrote to

---

[53] George Woodbine, Orders of July 22, 1814, Cochrane Papers (Directed to Lt. Smith and signed at Prospect Bluff).
[54] Please see Dale Cox, *Nicolls' Outpost*, Bascom, 2015.

a Mr. Mumford in Milledgeville on August 5 reporting that two men from Cheaha had arrived the previous evening with news that a raid was coming:

> ...[F]our men from the hostile partey that has joined the British was seen by a Chehaw man crossing the Flint river at the old field where the old Chehaw town was formerly. The Chehaw man asked him where they were goeing. There answer was to Ockmulge. They were asked if their business was to steal horses. Their answer was that was not the whole they meant to do.[55]

The site of the encounter was near Aumuccalee, the Cheaha town first described by Col. Hawkins in 1799. It stood in today's Lee County, Georgia, not far east of the original site of Fowltown. The Tutalosi were back on familiar ground and had already advanced to a point further north than any other British-affiliated force would reach from the Gulf Coast during the entire final campaign of the War of 1812.

---

[55] Timothy Barnard to Mr. Mumford, August 5, 1814, Hargrett Rare Book and Manuscript Library, The University of Georgia Libraries, Telamon Cuyler Collection, Box 01, Folder 11, Document 15.

5

THE WAR OF 1812

THE FIRST ATTACK AGAINST THE GEORGIA FRONTIER by the Tutalosis struck near Hartford, Georgia. Crossing the Flint River above the mouth of Kinchafoonee Creek, the warriors penetrated the white settlements along the Oconee and Ocmulgee Rivers. Timothy Barnard warned his friends there to be on their guard:

> …The man that saw them, he says he said every thing he could to stop them but to no purpose. They crossed the river and pushed on. Yesterday [August 4, 18114] was the fourth day since they crossed Flint river therefore I fear before this they have committed some murder or stole of some horses, perhaps both. The Aumauculle Chiefs has appointed seven men to way lay the river and if they return back the same way and bring horses, to take them from the robbers and have them sent to Hartford.[56]

Barnard's fears were realized on the same day as the penning of his warning. Lt. Col. Allen Tooke of the 35th Regiment, Georgia Militia,

---

[56] Timothy Barnard to Mr. Mumford, August 5, 1814.

reported to Gov. Peter Early on the following morning that the homes of settlers had been attacked not far from the fledgling town of Hartford:

> It is with great pain I have to communicate to your Excellency, that we had a very serious alarm from the Indians yesterday evening at three o'clock, in the field of Mr. John Rabun, which is between seven and eight miles below Hartford and immediately on the river – The said Rabun being in his field, three Indians arose out of the corn, and one of them fired on him and wounded him severely in the back – He immediately took to flight – The pursued him with the most horrid yells, and as he crossed the fence both the others fired on him and wounded him slightly in the shoulder. They continued to pursue him near his house, where he got his gun and would have fired on them but for the interference of his wife, who clung around him and prevented him.[57]

The attack at Rabun's farm was followed by additional raids at two nearby homes. No one else was injured but the warriors plundered the families of anything they could use and also made off with a horse belonging to John Bolling. A red war club was found on the ground where Rabun had been attacked. Lt. Col. Tooke called out detachments from his regiment to pursue the raiding party but no success was achieved in finding them. He also sent lieutenant's commands to occupy Forts Pike, Mitchell and Green "to protect the defenceless frontier of this county." The second of these stockades should not be confused with the post of the same name on the Chattahoochee River in what is now Russell County, Alabama.[58]

---

[57] Lt. Col. Allen Tooke to Gov. Peter Early, August 6, 1814, printed in the *Georgia Journal*, August 10, 1814.
[58] *Ibid.*

The raid by the Fowltown warriors marked the beginning of a fall and winter of predatory warfare on the Georgia frontier. They were joined in these attacks by other groups, particularly from the new Okitiyakana and Yuchi towns west of the Chattahoochee in today's Jackson County, Florida. The warriors readying themselves to go to war against the United States and the Big Warrior faction of the Creeks ranged in age from young teens to elderly men. They were still hungry despite the flood of supplies that the British were flooding up the Apalachicola River and many had lost family members in addition livestock, possessions, their homes, fields and more. They were especially impressed by the new muskets and bayonets that were being provided to them. "He appeared particularly pleased with his musket and bayonet," Lt. Col. Nicolls wrote of an elderly Red Stick who he met during his first brief visit to Prospect Bluff, "and observed that he always thought something was wanting, for that while the enemy was loading, and he was loading, much time was lost, that now he had a bayonet he would rush on the American, when he was sure of victory."[59]

Col. Benjamin Hawkins responded to the raid near Hartford by instructing William McIntosh to capture the arms and ammunition being stockpiled on the Apalachicola and lower Chattahoochee Rivers. The Coweta chief now bore the rank of major thanks to his service at Horseshoe Bend and elsewhere during the Creek War. Reports spread across the frontier in September that McIntosh had marched on the British depots and allied villages. Hawkins confirmed that a force of 196 warriors had left Coweta on September 23 in route to the lower towns. They were joined by 100-200 more men along the way.[60]

The strike force led by Maj. McIntosh stopped first at Eufaula:

---

[59] Lt. Col. Edward Nicolls to Admiral Alexander Cochrane, August 12, 1814, Cochrane Papers.
[60] Col. Benjamin Hawkins to John Armstrong, Secretary of War, October 5, 1814, *American State Papers – Indian Affairs*, Volume I, page 861; *Georgia Journal*, September 7, 1814.

...On his arrival at Eufaulau he was informed the British officers with the runaway and stolen negro's had left the Seminolie Country for Pensacola. He continued his march notwithstanding to Perrymans square where all the Seminolie Chiefs were [gathered]. – They seemed surprised at his appearance in arms among them, assured him of their pacific disposition and wish to remain in peace and quietness with every body. They said the negro's in their country who had not gone to Pensacola had run into the Swamps to hide themselves. He might return home, all runaway negros which are in their country shall be hunted up and sent to their owners.[61]

The Fowltown chiefs and warriors, who lived directly across the river, were part of the gathering of leaders that McIntosh discovered when he arrived at Perryman's town. They could not have been happy about the presence of the major and his Creek soldiers in their community or with his decision to leave behind two chiefs to "observe" them when he withdrew a few days later. Once they knew that McIntosh was gone, the chiefs convened a council of a different sort:

The Seminoles have had a gathering at Perryman's for mischief. They are making their war-food. They have received orders from the British to make ready, and to strike on this side without delay when the British are ready to strike on the other. They were to be ready by this full moon. A large party was soon after this full moon to march off some where for mischief, supposed the frontiers of Georgia below Fort-Hawkins and probably near Hartford. One of the informants says he heard several of them say they had been ill-treated near

---

[61] Col. Benjamin Hawkins to Gov. Peter Early, October 12, 1814, Telamon Cuyler Collection, Hargrett Rare Book and Manuscript Library, The University of Georgia Libraries, Box 76, Boulder 25, Document 10.

Hartford, and the day was not far off when they would be revenged.[62]

Col. Hawkins learned of this second gathering from multiple sources and immediately ordered his assistant agent, Christian Limbaugh, to raise as many warriors as possible to garrison the empty forts along the frontier until white troops could arrive.

Events now began to happen with surprising rapidity. Lt. Col. Nicolls, who commanded the growing British force in Florida, outlined his plans in a report written in early November 1814:

> ...My intention now is to throw up strong works at the Bluff. I have written for cannon and stores, to Governor Cameron. I shall continue to raise as many men as I can, in order to be ready for whatever expedition you may order. From present appearances I think it probable, by the time you want them, I can have 4500 Indians ready to embark, on any service in the Gulf, and plenty to guard or even attack from their own neighbourhood. They entreat me to build two forts, one at the bluff, and the other at the point of land formed by the Flint and Chatahatchee rivers. This is I think a reasonable request, as they say if you take us away you ought to have a protection for our wives and children. The red sticks have behaved (with a very few exceptions) entirely to my satisfaction.[63]

---

[62] Col. Benjamin Hawkins to Gov. Peter Early, October 30, 1814, published in the *Georgia Journal*, November 2, 1814.

[63] Lt. Col. Edward Nicolls to Admiral Alexander Cochrane, August 12, 1814 – November 1814, Cochrane Papers. This section of the report appears to have been written on November 13, 1814.

Nicolls informed Admiral Alexander Cochrane that he hoped to establish peace between the Red Sticks and the Big Warrior soon and anticipated that he would "enter Georgia with a strong hand." He did not know that Cochrane's fleet was on its way to Apalachicola Bay where it would stop prior to the planned attack on New Orleans.[64]

Word once again went up the Flint River that British-allied warriors from Fowltown and other villages were preparing to advance on the Georgia frontier. Timothy Barnard, however, cited Jack Kinnard as the source for information that the planned attack had once again been cancelled:

> My son Timpuge [i.e. Timpoochee] arrived here yesterday from his route to Chehaw and old Kenard told my son that he had an express come to him that the war Indians were on their march which alarmed him a good deal which caused him to have an express sent to you. Kenerd relates that the day after this happ. Five of the Aumauculle Chiefs that had been down at the mouth of the rivers where Perriman lives arrived at their town and informed Kenerd that the war party had stopped coming on in consequence of which Kenerd requested of my son to proceed on up to your house and give you the information.[65]

The chief of Aumuccalee sent word via Timpoochee Barnard that he and his warriors would not join the Red Sticks in their planned attack. He asked the younger Barnard to inform Col. Hawkins that they would join with the whites in resisting the British, but that he would need help because he did not know how his people could survive on their own if

---

[64] *Ibid.*

[65] Timothy Barnard to Col. Benjamin Hawkins, November 3, 1814 (apparently written on November 2, 1814), Hargrett Rare Book and Manuscript Libraries, The University of Georgia Libraries, Telamon Cuyler Collection, Box 01, Folder 11, Document 16.

they evacuated their town. Timpoochee's father credited an Aumuccalee chief named "Hitchufalawa" got convincing the Tutalosi warriors and their allies from carrying out an immediate attack. He hoped that Georgians would use the time thus gained:

> It may give our frontier inhabitants time to be better prepared. It seems the British officer that was up at Perimans at the time urging the Red Stick on was much offended at the red people not proceeding on the route. He and Perriman pushed on down to the stores at the mouth of the river. Should not have wrote you so much as my son was going up by request of the chiefs to tell you all the news but expected you might be gone in to Fort Hawkins. Am still in so low a state am scarcely able to sit up to write or to walk about. My son can tell you about your runaway black. He says when he got down to Aumaucule that there was but very few red people in the town. The Wolf Warrior at the time was laying very sick. The first and only news he could hear of them was that they were seen ten miles off from the east side of the river twenty miles below Obaunes.[66]

The warning from the two Barnards was reinforced by runners from other Lower Creek towns as they arrived at Fort Hawkins with the news that a major offensive by the British-allied warriors was expected. Col. Hawkins wrote to Gov. Peter Early from the fort on the morning of November 3, promising to do all within his power to use the warriors enrolled under his command to protect the frontier. He believed that the best way to do this with a preemptive strike down the Chattahoochee:

> I shall make Cowetau my head quarters and act from thence as circumstances may require. I shall order all the

---

[66] *Ibid.*

Uchees to embody under Capt. Barnard and station them 20 miles below Fort Lawrence. I shall give a like order to the Chiefs of Aumuccullee to remain 30 miles lower still to reconnoiter the movement of the enemy. From Cowetau I can defend the posts, which it is desirable they should attack in preference of your frontiers. If the militia officers in the agency will cooperate under my command with a little aid from you we will soon make the enemy retrace his steps with loss. I shall want 100 mounted infantry. It is bad policy and will never do to act defensively against Indians on a frontier as extensive as yours. On the appearance of hostility they must be traced up to their towns and crushed. The reason is favorable and what provision they have made is ready for us. As they have manifested hostility and made a movement towards us. If the Chiefs of Aumuccullee should prevail on them to desist it will be but temporary as the British force will be ready to act with them. We had better begin and act with effect against them.[67]

Hawkins informed Early that he knew that the governor was facing many calls for militia so he would attempt to carry out the proposed campaign with as little support as possible. If 500 mounted Georgians could join him, he believed that the united column could "crush those people."[68]

A flurry of messages were exchanged between the agent and the governor over the next two days as they discussed the logistics for the campaign. Before Hawkins could leave for Cusseta, however, news arrived from "Carr's Ned (a free black man who speaks the Creek tongue well, and is deemed a man of truth)" that a large force of enemy warriors

---

[67] Col. Benjamin Hawkins to Gov. Peter Early, November 3, 1814, Hargrett Rare Book and Manuscript Library, The University of Georgia Libraries, Telamon Cuyler Collection, Box 76, Folder 25, Document 12.
[68] *Ibid.*

had been seen near Hartford. They took Ned prisoner but he convinced them that he was on his way to join the British so they let him go.[69]

It is still unclear whether the warriors encountered by Ned were actually planning an attack. No raids took place and they may have been on a reconnoitering expedition. Fowltown warriors were probably part of the party since they constantly operated in the vicinity. Gov. Early took no chances and prepared the frontier for defense:

> On the receipt of the above information [i.e. Ned's report], orders were instantly issued by the Governor to Col. Tooke of Pulaski, directing him to use all the means in his powers "for repeling, pursuing and destroying any such hostile party;" and for this purpose, captain Thomas's troop of horse, previously ordered out, has been required to cooperate. Col. Wimberly, of Twiggs, has likewise been directed to call out a rifle and cavalry company to co-operate with Col. Tooke. For the better security of the frontier, the whole of the first class of militia in Pulaski, and of the frontier districts in Twiggs, have been discharged from the orders heretofore given for their marching to Mobile.[70]

Maj. Cook reported from Fort Hawkins on November 7 that he had requested Col. Jones of Jones County to order out part of his militia regiment without delay. Hawkins, he reported, had just left the fort for the Creek Agency on the Flint with plans to move as quickly as possible with the warriors who were assembling per his instructions. If supported by the anticipated reinforcements from the Georgia Militia, the agent would "endeavor to get the enemy's rear." Gov. Early supported Cook's request by order Jones to call out his regiment. Additional militia troops were also ordered out in Twiggs County under Col. Wimberly.[71]

---

[69] Col. Benjamin Hawkins to Gov. Peter Early, November 5, 1814, published in the *Georgia Journal*, November 9, 1814.

[70] *Georgia Journal*, November 9, 1814.

Andrew Jackson took Pensacola on the same day, driving out the British. The Red Sticks had already crossed Pensacola Bay to safety and were on their way across the Florida Panhandle to the Apalachicola and lower Chattahoochee Rivers. The British military forces skirmished briefly with Jackson's army before evacuating the city to their ships. The magazines of the fort of San Carlos de Barrancas were intentionally exploded and the Cuban garrison there forced by the British to evacuate with them. Jackson withdrew back to Mobile after having enjoyed the sight of his enemies ships as they sailed away.

Nicolls and Woodbine returned to the Apalachicola where they soon began to build a new fort on the east bank of the river one mile below the forks of the Chattahoochee and Flint. This post – usually called Nicolls' Outpost today – was intended to serve as a base for operations against Georgia. The warriors of Fowltown soon relocated there to join with other forces in preparing for operations on a larger scale. Whether their families went with them and their village opposite Perryman's town was abandoned is not known. No evidence of its occupation after November 1814 can be found.

---

[71] *Ibid.*

6

"CHASTISE THE FOULE TOWN PEOPLE"

COLONEL BENJAMIN HAWKINS moved from the Creek Agency on the Flint to Coweta on the Chattahoochee in November 1814. The climactic moments of the War of 1812 in the Gulf Coast region were at hand. A key part of the war from the American point of view was a campaign against the Native American towns and British forts on the lower Chattahoochee, Flint and Apalachicola Rivers.

The campaign began with a deliberate effort to pressure the Lower Creek towns north of Eufaula on the Chattahoochee and around Aumuccalee ("Chehaw") on the Flint into joining the attack on the British and their allies. A council was held at Coweta where the Little Prince threw down the gauntlet against such of his own people – Cusseta among them - as were trying to remain neutral in the conflict:

> You have now heard the Talks – all who are not willing to protect their own nation will be considered hostile to the United States – I have thrown away the Seminoles – we shall now have to go to war against them. I do not understand what you Cussetaus are about, or what you intend. You must say quickly what you

mean to do – there is no time to be considering on it now
– If you are for the British say so.[72]

The assembled chiefs agreed to join the United States in its war
against the British and their allies from Perryman's town, Fowltown,
Okitiyakani and elsewhere. Timpoochee Barnard, now a captain under
Hawkins, quickly put 80 of the Yuchis – mostly from the Flint River –
into the field to scout any threatened movements by the enemy. Several
"Seminoles" – probably Lower Creeks either Fowltown or Okitiyakani –
drew next blood however, proving that the British force also had spies of
its own watching the Georgia frontier:

> Three Seminole Indians went a few days ago to Fort
> Lawrence and delivered themselves up, saying they
> belonged to one of the parties lately on our frontier, and
> had been compelled to flee for safety in consequence of
> an affray with some British soldiers who were along....
> [T]he commanding officer determined to send them to
> Fort Hawkins for further examination, and accordingly
> started them off with a guard of three men. The Indians
> were permitted to loiter along the road till night, when at
> a signal they rose on the guard, wounded one of them
> severely with a knife, and effected their escape.[73]

U.S. authorities concluded that the "surrendering" warriors were
spies who used a ruse to scout the strength of Fort Lawrence, a post on
the Federal Road between Fort Hawkins and the Chattahoochee River. It
was located in today's Taylor County, Georgia. Other reports flooded in
with the news that the British were building a fort just below the forks of
the Chattahoochee and Flint Rivers and that the Red Sticks and other
British-allied Native Americans were concentrating there.[74]

---

[72] Talk of the Little Prince, published in the *Georgia Journal*, November 23,
1814.
[73] *Georgia Journal*, November 23, 1814.

The officers of the Georgia militia clearly blamed Fowltown for the raids that had been taking place along the Georgia frontier. Most of these resulted in livestock being taken but no injuries or deaths to settlers, a sign that the Tutalosis were abiding by their agreement with Capt. George Woodbine to follow British rules of war. A report that several of Neamathla's warriors had been seen crossing the Flint River near Aumuccalee – which the Georgians consistently called "Chehaws" – led Lt. Col. Allen Tooke to lead a force of 150 militia troops down to the village to investigate. He was joined by Capt. Barnard and some of his Yuchis as he approached the town, while the rest of the Native American officer's warriors continued on to Hartford for resupply:

> ...I understood that three Indians supposed to be hostile were seen the day before I reached Chehaw a few miles below that Town aiming for the Ocmulgee and enquiring for Col. Hawkins'. I asked about it and they denied it at first but soon finding that I knew the fact too well for it to be disputed they admitted it. I then insisted on their detaching some of the young men in pursuit of them and pursue them until they overtook them. At first some of the chiefs appeared willing but after some debate they refused. I mentioned our cutting a road through their country on to the Fork of the Rivers. They made no reply.[75]

The chiefs of Aumuccalee did agree to send a delegation down the Flint to negotiate with the leaders of the pro-British forces in hopes of stalling a general advance against the frontier. Lt. Col. Tooke reported that even the warriors that he believed would support Georgia and the

---

[74] *Ibid.*
[75] Lt. Col. Allen Tooke to Gov. Peter Early, November 21, 1814, Hargrett Rare Books and Manuscripts Library, The University of Georgia Libraries, Telamon Cuyler Collection, Box 47, Folder 04, Document 07.

United States, were "well supplied with British muskets and ammunition which they acknowledged to have drawn from the British down at Perryman's."[76]

The British also received an account of the appearance of the Georgia Militia at Aumuccalee, as Lt. Col. Nicolls described to Admiral Cochrane on December 3, 1814:

> ...The Brother of the Foule Town Chief is just arrived, he says two hundred enemey's cavalry came into the Chief's town and asked their leave to [attack] and chastise the Foule Town people for stealing their Horses, but unfortunately they would not let them. If they had the Foule Town people would have brought them down to me. The Chehaws are but lately armed and they are very faithful.[77]

Nicolls seems to have been confused as to the identities of both the individual who arrived at Prospect Bluff and the chief of Aumuccalee. Circumstances indicate that the "brother of the Foule Town Chief" was probably Neamathla, the actual Fowltown chief. The chief of Aumuccullee, an individual called "Old Howard" by the whites, may have been a brother of Neamathla. He is definitely known to have been an uncle of the Coweta war chief William McIntosh. If he was also related to Neamathla, then the encounter reveals much about the confusing "brother against brother" nature of the Creek War and War of 1812 in the Southeast. Lt. Col. Nicolls also confirmed that the weapons and ammunition seen by Lt. Col. Tooke on the Flint River had been provided by the British.[78]

---

[76] *Ibid.*

[77] Lt. Col. Edward Nicolls to Admiral Alexander Cochrane, December 3, 1814, Cochrane Papers.

[78] *Ibid.*

Nicolls' confirmation that the warriors accused of raiding the Georgia frontier were from "Foule Town" clearly shows the degree to which Neamathla and his men had committed themselves to the British war effort. The warriors from the towns of Thomas and William Perryman remained largely on the defensive, but the Tutalosis were activity engaged in harassing the frontier. In addition to gather intelligence and livestock, they also assisted maroons (escaped slaves) in reaching the British posts on the Apalachicola. Nicolls and Woodbine were actively recruiting black soldiers for the battalion of Colonial Marines being organized at Prospect Bluff. Slaves claimed by Jack Kinnard and even Col. Hawkins himself were among those who reached Spanish Florida with help from the British-allied warriors.

A key moment in the British efforts to build an army for the invasion of Georgia came near the end of the first week of December 1814. The main British fleet arrived off Apalachicola Bay and Admiral Alexander Cochrane joined Gen. John Keane in issuing a proclamation to the leaders and warriors of the "Creek and other Indian Nations." The admiral's flagship, HMS *Tonnant*, carried a printing press and the call for support is believed to have been the first document ever printed in Florida:

> Hear! O ye brave Chiefs of the Creek and other Indian Nations.
>
> The great King George, our beloved father, has long wished to assuage the sorrows of his warlike Indian children, and to assist them in gaining their rights and possessions from their base and perfidious oppressors.
>
> The trouble our father has had in conquering his enemies beyond the great waters, he has brought to a glorious conclusion; and peace is again restored amongst all the nations of Europe.
>
> The desire, therefore, which he has long felt, of assisting you, and the assurance which he has given you

of his powerful protection, he has now chosen as is chiefs by sea and land to carry into effectual execution.

Know then, O Chiefs and Warriors, that in obedience to the Great Spirit which directs the soul of our Mighty Father, we come with a power which it were vain for all the people of the United States to oppose. Behold the great waters covered with our ships, from which will go forth an army of warriors, as numerous as the whole Indian nations; inured to the toils and hardships of war – accustomed to triumph over all opposition – the constant favourites of victory.

The same principle of justice which le dour father to wage a war of 20 years in favour of the oppressed nations of Europe, animates him now in support of his Indian children; and by the efforts of his warriors, he hopes to obtain for them the restoration of those lands of which the people of the bad spirit have lately robbed them.

We promised you by our talk of last June, that great fleets and armies were coming to attack our foes : and you will have heard of our having triumphantly taken their capital city of Washington, as well as many other places – beaten their armies in battle, and spread terror over the heart of their country.

Come forth then, ye brave chiefs and warriors, as one family, and join the British standard – the signal of union between the powerful and oppressed – the symbol of justice, led on by victory.

If you want covering to protect yourselves, your wives and your children, against the winter's cold, - come to us, and we will cloth you. If you want arms and ammunition to defend yourselves against your oppressors, - come to us, and we will provide you. Call around you the whole of your Indian brethren – and we will show them the same tokens of our brotherly love.

And what think you we ask in return for this bounty of our Great Father, which we his chosen warriors have so much pleasure in offering to you? Nothing more than that you should assist us manfully in regaining your lost lands – the lands of your forefathers – from the common enemy, the people of the United States; and that you should hand down these lands to your children hereafter, as we hope we shall now be able to deliver them up to you, we have forced our enemies to ask for a peace, our good Father will on no account forget the welfare of his much-lov'd Indian children.

Again then, brave Chiefs, and warriors of the Indian nation, at the mandate of the Great Spirit, we call upon you to come forth arrayed in battle to fight the great fight of justice, and recover your long-lost freedom. Animate your hearts in this sacred cause – unite with us as the sons of one common father, - and a great and glorious victory will shortly crown our exertions.
Given under our hands and seals on board his Brittanic Majesty's ship Tonnant, off Appalachicolo.

ALEX. COCHRANE.

JOHN KEANE.

Dec. 5, 1814.[79]

Not all of the British were as enlightened in their views of the Creeks as Lt. Col. Nicolls, Adm. Cochrane and Gen. Keane. Sir Edward Codrington, for example, attended a dinner aboard the *Tonnant* with Thomas Perryman, Cappachimico, Josiah Francis and others. He was not impressed:

---

[79] Adm. Alex. Cochrane and Gen. John Keane to the Great and Illustrious Chiefs of the Creek and other Indian Nations, December 5, 1814, republished in *The Times of London*, August 15, 1818.

...I find I have not yet, however, mentioned to you the arrival of our magnanimous allies Kings Capichi and Hopsy (or Perriman), with their upper and second warriors, the Prophet Francis, Helis Hadjo, the ambassador from the Big Warrior, &c., &c. We had the honour of these Majestic Beasts dining with us two days in the 'Tonnant,' and we are to be disgusted with a similar honour here to-day. All the body clothes they get they put on one over the other, except trowsers, which they consider as encumbrances it should seem in our way of using them, and they therefore tie them round their waists for the present, in order to convert them into leggings hereafter. Some of them appeared in their own picturesque dresses at first, with the skin of a handsome plumed bird on the head and arms; the bird's beak pointing down the forehead, the wings over the ears, and the tail down the poll. But they are now all in hats (some cocked, gold-laced ones), and in jackets such as are worn by sergeants in the Guards, and they have now the appearance of dressed-up apes.[80]

The arrival of the British fleet off Apalachicola saved the Georgia frontier from impending attack. Nicolls and most of his marines went aboard the transports, as did Cappachimico, Francis, Thomas Perryman and others. They were on hand for the British invasion of Louisiana and the Battle of New Orleans, including Jackson's stunning victory of January 8, 1815. The forces left on the Apalachicola and lower Chattahoochee and Flint Rivers continued to strengthen their positions and distribute arms. Neamathla and the Fowltown warriors maintained their toward the Georgia frontier, watching for signs of enemy movements and engaging in occasional raids.

---

[80] Edward Codrington to his Daughter, December 14, 1814, *Memoir of the Life of Admiral Sir Edward Codrington*, page 239.

Maj. Gen. John McIntosh – who should not be confused with the Coweta war chief Maj. William McIntosh – commanded the Georgia militia that had been called out due to the British threat. The *Georgia Journal* reported on December 8 that he had ordered his men to begin building boats on the Chattahoochee River for the expected campaign down to Perryman's town and Fowltown. The vessels would be used to carry troops and supplies. Additional instructions were handed down on the next day by the governor, who ordered McIntosh to march to Mobile with a portion of his command. Maj. Gen. Andrew Jackson correctly deduced that a British attack on either Mobile or New Orleans – or both – was imminent and had called on Georgia for support. A second column of Georgia troops under Brig. Gen. David Blackshear was instructed to march from Hartford to the Flint River near Aumuccalee. This force was to build a new fort on the Flint and then move downstream to cooperate with the Creek brigade under Col. Hawkins in an attack that would also include Miccosukee.[81]

Maj. Samuel Dale, the famed Mississippi partisan, arrived at the Creek Agency on the Flint on December 11, 1814, with news that a large British flight had been sighted off the mouth of the Mississippi River. Andrew Jackson had headed for New Orleans for New Orleans and almost all of the infantry west of the Creek Nation was also marching in that direction. A force under Maj. Uriah Blue of the 39th U.S. Infantry, however, was launching a campaign in the opposite direction:

> Maj. Blue with about fifteen or sixteen hundred mounted men, Choctaw, Chickasaw & Creeks were to march on the 1st inst. for Apalachicola, in pursuit of the Red Sticks and their allies. He was to use wagons as far as practicable for the transportation of provisions then dismount 200 or more if necessary of his men and use

---

[81] *Georgia Journal*, December 8, 1814; Gov. Peter Early to Maj. Gen. John McIntosh, December 9, 1814, Governor's Letter Book B, Georgia Department of Archives and History, pp. 56-57.

their horses as pack horses. Lieut. Carey of the United States Army, and his associates three men, a woman and a child passing on westwardly are missing. They left Fort Jackson by water. The woman and child have been massacred in the streets of Pensacola, having only time to state she was of this party, and that the men were killed.[82]

The column under Maj. Blue was to push through the Florida Panhandle to the Apalachicola while the Creek Brigade under Col. Hawkins came down the Chattahoochee River and a brigade of Georgia militia under Brig. Gen. Blackshear descended the Flint. These forces would concentrate near the forks of the Chattahoochee and Flint. Combined, they would provide an impressive army of nearly 3,000 men. They would destroy the British forts on the Apalachicola, the towns of Perryman, Neamathla and other chiefs who were in arms against the United States, and then march on Miccosukee.

---

[82] Maj. Gen. John McIntosh to Gov. Peter Early, December 14, 1814, Hargrett Rare Book and Manuscript Library, The University of Georgia Libraries, Telamon Cuyler, Box 47, Folder 04, Document 09.

7

THE HAWKINS' CAMPAIGN

COLONEL BENJAMIN HAWKINS' CAMPAIGN against the British and Native American forces at the forks of the Chattahoochee and Flint Rivers began to take shape even as Lt. Col. Edward Nicolls and many of his men withdrew to take part in the attack on New Orleans. Neamathla and his warriors were at Nicolls' Outpost, the new fort on the Apalachicola about one mile below the forks. The northernmost post built by the British during their Gulf Coast Campaign, this earthen redoubt stood at a complex of prehistoric Native American mounds. Its location served to elevate it above the normal winter flood stage of the Apalachicola River and it was close enough to control navigation of the forks with cannon fire. It was also across the line in Spanish Florida. It is not known if the women, children and elderly of Fowltown moved to the outpost at the same time as the men, but it seems unlikely that Neamathla would have left them in a town 10 miles up the Chattahoochee where they could be attacked and captured should the Coweta return down the river.

The arrival of Admiral Cochrane's fleet off Apalachicola Bay served to confuse American authorities as to the strength and location of the British invasion force. Slow communications caused news of the presence of the ships there to reach officials in Georgia at the same time as the first reports of the arrival of the fleet of the Belize or mouth of the

Mississippi River. The initial fear was that so many enemy troops had come that British commanders would be able to attack New Orleans, Mobile and the Georgia frontier simultaneously. These fears were further exacerbated because yet another invasion force had reached the waters off Cumberland Island on the Georgia coast.

The appearance of so many enemy sails in so many places almost caused the plan campaign down the Chattahoochee and Flint Rivers to fall apart before it could be launched. Maj. Gen. John McIntosh assumed command at Mobile after marching his force of Georgia militia through the Creek Nation from Fort Mitchell on the Chattahoochee River. Realizing that a British fleet could easily take the city if it blasted its way past Fort Bowyer on Mobile Point, he immediately called for additional troops and Col. Hawkins' expectation that white soldiers would join in his movement down the Chattahoochee quickly evaporated.

Hawkins rightly feared that the frontier could come under major attack if his campaign was delayed but took solace in the fact that Brig. Gen. David Blackshear's brigade of Georgia militia troops would still descend the Flint River to join him at the forks. Whether the combined force of the two columns could have dealt with the force that the British had assembled on the Apalachicola is another matter. Even after the withdrawal of Nicolls and many of the troops for the New Orleans attack, British officers reported that 3,551 warriors and soldiers were assembled below the international border. These included 170 black Colonial Marine recruits, 760 Miccosukee and Seminole warriors, 400 "Chihaw" warriors (a number that probably included the Fowltown and Okitiyakani men), 800 Red Stick Creeks and 1,421 Lower Creek waters called out by Thomas Perryman from the towns south of Eufaula. The combined U.S. force would number approximately half as many men.

The American agent never fully realized the strength of the army opposing him. He did receive occasional intelligence from downriver thanks to his practice of sending Creek warriors into the British camps as spies. In January 1815, for example, he added the latest information from the Apalachicola when he reported to Maj. Gen. McIntosh that a party of Miccosukee had struck exposed settlements east of the Flint River:

The chief warrior of Mic,co,soo,kee led a party of his warriors towards the frontiers of Georgia, ten in number, and killed five white people, and carried the scalps to the British below the confluence of the Flint and Chattahoochie. There are a few white troops at Forbes's store (18 miles up the Apalachicola on the East side). The store was surrounded with a ditch. 32 warriors of Choctaws from Fort Jackson (a part of those who had surrendered there) and a great many red clubs were there. The runaway and stolen negroes were close by the store; Provision short, bisquit only. So great the scarcity of meat that the Choctaws subsisted partly on old stinking cow hides.

The supplies of Indian goods, arms and ammunition very abundant. Two houses of dry goods and four of saddles, brass kettles, arms and ammunition. There were some vessels back of the Islands opposite the mouth of the river, with troops on board, and some of the troops were landed and could be seen from the mouth of the river.[83]

Hawkins, like many white Americans, never recognized the black men on the Apalachicola River as soldiers. This was a serious mistake on their part. The maroons and free blacks who had joined Nicolls and Woodbine were members of the British Colonial Marines. They were well-armed, well-equipped and many of them had been in training for at least five months. They underwent drills in musketry, marines tactics and artillery. Food shortages were chronic at the British posts but enough trickled in to keep the men, women and children there alive. With 3,551 soldiers and warriors on the river – excluding white British troops – the

---

[83] Col. Benjamin Hawkins to Maj. Gen. John McIntosh, January 4, 1815, Hargrett Rare Book and Manuscript Library, The University of Georgia Libraries, Telamon Cuyler Collection, Box 76, Folder 25, Document 18.

number of noncombatants protected at the forts must have been astronomical.

Maj. Gen. McIntosh was still at Fort Mitchell when Hawkins penned his report but he informed Gov. Early on the same day that he was preparing to march. He apparently had considered withdrawing Blackshear's column from the campaign down the rivers but decided against it:

> ...Weighing all the circumstances, and the distance I am placed from Genl. Blackshear, and the improbability of his being timely to render services in the present urgent call at Mobile, I have determined to direct him to pursue the object of subduing any hostile tribes of Indians over (or) British in that quarter – which, when effected, to follow me to Mobile. Colo. will cooperate heartily with him in the defeat of the Indians or British in that quarter and will leave this for the fork of the Chattahoochee and Flint rivers about the 9th inst. with seven hundred Indians, fine fellows, heartily engaged in our cause.

The "Colo." referred to in the letter was of course Benjamin Hawkins. Enough boats were nearing completion for much of his force to move by water down the Chattahoochee River. The rest of the warriors would move by land, scouting the lands between the Chattahoochee and Flint as they moved.

McIntosh also reported that part of Maj. Uriah Blue's column had arrived at Fort Decatur on the Tallapoosa River. He did not mention or probably know it, but this force included the famed frontiersman David Crockett, who later wrote about the expedition into West Florida. According to Crockett, the Tennessee and Choctaw soldiers under Maj. Blue captured or killed a number of Red Stick warriors but ran out of food before they could reach the Apalachicola. The attacked the camp of a Red Stick chief named Holmes – probably the chief referred to as

"Homes" by Woodbine and Hawkins – near the Choctawhatchee River only to find it empty. The inhabitants had evacuated leaving little food behind them. Blue had hoped to find supplies in the village and was forced to divide his column and begin a miserable and hungry withdrawal. One wing of his force – Crockett and the other Tennesseans included – headed north for the Creek Nation while Blue and the Choctaws retreated back to the Tensaw settlements north of Mobile. The first of the three columns in the U.S. campaign against the British and Native American forces on the Apalachicola had failed to achieve its objective.[84]

Col. Hawkins did not know it, but the second column under Gen. Blackshear was also at risk. Rumors were growing of a planned British invasion of St. Marys and Cumberland Island. Enemy boats had been spotted at Sapelo Island and British ships were reported to be off Amelia Island. The civilian population was nervous and it was not long before they began to protest the withdrawal of Blackshear and his men from their area for the campaign on the Flint:

> I am requested by a large portion of the Inhabitants of this [i.e. McIntosh] County, as their Representative to pray your Excellency, to countermand, the order for the marching of the Detachment to the Indian frontier, it is the opinion of the whole County, that, we have nothing to fear from Indian invasion, as they have sufficient employment at home, whilst our whole Sea Coast has much to apprehend from British spoliation. Those men now under orders to march; are drafted from the Sea Coast, leaving their families and property completely exposed.[85]

---

[84] See David Crockett, *A Narrative of the Life of David Crockett of Tennessee.*

[85] Rep. Francis Hopkins to Gov. Peter Early, January 10, 1815, Hargrett Rare Book and Manuscript Library, The University of Georgia Libraries, Telamon Cuyler Collection, Box 77, Folder 30, Document 13.

The fears of the residents of McIntosh County proved founded. British troops descended on Cumberland Island just three days later:

> We have at length certain accounts of the enemy having landed at Cumberland Island. An express passed through this place to-day, at 2 o'clock, P.M. for Camp Covington, addressed to Gen. Floyd, from Capt. Massias, the commanding officer at Point Petre. By the express we have learnt the following particulars – that the enemy landed on Tuesday and Wednesday last in two divisions, one at Plum Orchard and the other at Dungeness, in thirty barges, containing about two thousand men, blacks and whites. A great part of the fleet (8 or 10 vessels) were off St. Andrew's bar, and many of their barges were within that bar on Thursday last. Two or three of the British barges attempted to pass the fort at Point Petre, but were fired on and compelled to retreat. It is not yet known how many troops they have actually with them, or what their intentions are – we think that it is the van of a force destined against the southern coast, which in all probability will desolate the sea islands between this and St. Mary's, and then make an attack on Savannah: To-Morrow we shall be able to give a further and more particular account.[86]

The British soon took both St. Marys and the American battery at Point Peter (also spelled Point Petre). Both sides suffered casualties but Capt. A.A. Massias and his small force from the U.S. Rifle Regiment had no chance against the overwhelming British force of Admiral George Cockburn. St. Marys was looted and most of its citizens forced to flee. The U.S. troops in the region began to assemble on the north bank of the

---

[86] *Savannah Republican*, January 15, 1815, 8 p.m.

Altamaha but their officers knew that without reinforcements they could not hope to stop the British.[87]

Brig. Gen. Blackshear, meanwhile, advanced to Hartford and from there began the laborious work of opening a new road to the Flint River. The road struck the river just north of Cedar Creek in present-day Crisp County, Georgia. The militia soldiers started the construction of a supply depot – often described as a "breastworks" – on higher ground overlooking the river. Many writers have placed the later Fort Early on the site of Blackshear's works, but the original fort was actually a short distance north of the later one. The Georgia militia's part of the campaign ended there. Orders were received from Gov. Early instructing Blackshear to withdraw from the Flint and march as quickly as possible for the Altamaha to counter the British invasion on the Atlantic seaboard. The troops withdrew from the Flint and the second of the three columns expected to converge on the forks of the Chattahoochee and Flint withdrew from the campaign.

The fate of the American campaign now hinged on Col. Hawkins himself. Not aware that Blackshear's command had been ordered back to the coast, he went forward with his part of the plan and left Fort Mitchell in early February 1815. He learned along the way of the British had invaded the Georgia coast and of the orders instructing Gen. Blackshear to assist in the defense of the state, but still expected that a different militia force would be sent down the Flint:

> …I only know incidentally that a British force is come against your seacoast, that General Blackshear was ordered there, And it may be General Clark also. On this supposition I have to state to you the President has accepted my resignation of the agency for Indian affairs, and Mr. Limbaugh is to take charge of them till a successor is appointed. Of course if General Clark does

---

[87] Letters from St. Mary's, January 18, 1815, published in the *American Telegraph*, February 15, 1815.

not come, with the cooperating force, a man of skill and abilities should be selected. I shall continue in the present crisis of our affairs until such a man arrives, or in the possible event of my receiving a commission to command the enrolled Indians.[88]

The colonel's hopes of reinforcements from Georgia would be dashed and no men would come down the Flint River to assist him. The total strength of his own column was variously stated as 700 or 1,000 men, much smaller than the 3,551 warriors that the British reported to have enrolled on the Apalachicola. Hawkins did not realize it, but he was placing himself in a very dangerous situation.

The boats from Fort Mitchell navigated the Chattahoochee River without difficulty. Hawkins reported that the river was "fine for boating" and that he did not encounter any obstructions on his way down to the border area. He reached a point that he estimated to be 112 miles below Fort Mitchell in just a few days and halted there to establish his camp. His scouts warned him that the British were strongly fortified just below the forks of the rivers:

> The Hostile force below the forks of the Rivers on the East of apalatchecola are about 300 who have entrenched themselves have a breast work abt. 4 feet high and One Howitzer and one Cohorn. They have 100 whites, 80 blacks and the remainder Indians. They are endeavouring by all the means in their power to increase their force with Simenolies & There is a Spanish officer among them whos rank I know not from Pensacola, Hugh McGill with some colored people. He ordered a Half breed my informant, who knew him well, out of their fort as being opposed to him and the British.[89]

---

[88] Col. Benjamin Hawkins to Gov. Peter Early, February 12, 1815, Hargrett Rare Book and Manuscript Library, The University of Georgia Libraries, Telamon Cuyler Collection, Box 76, Folder 25, Document 20.

Hugh McGill, mentioned in Hawkins' report of February 12, 1815, was a former sergeant in the U.S. Army who had deserted and joined the British Colonial Marines.

The artillery at Nicolls' Outpost was more powerful than might be suspected. The howitzer was a light 5 ½ inch gun that weighed roughly 1,700 pounds (carriage included). It fired a 5 ½ inch explosive shell with impressive accuracy at ranges of up to 800 yards. Accuracy varied past that point. The shells burst into as many as 20-30 jagged pieces when they exploded, each of which could maim at a distance of up to 250 feet from the point of explosion. It could also fire case shot – called canister by American gunners – against advancing personnel at closer ranges. These loads consisted of tin cans filled with smaller balls that would spread out like shell of a shotgun upon firing. The howitzer was a state of the art gun for the time and was a fearsome anti-personnel weapon. The coehorn at the outpost was also an impressive weapon. Much larger than the small, portable mortars of the same name that are familiar to many reenactors of today, the British piece could fire 24-pound explosive shells. Designed to be moved and fired by a relatively small crew, the coehorn was a mortar designed for lobbing shells high into the air and then down through the decks of boats or bodies of men. It was generally considered most effective when used for close-range fire.

Hawkins does not seem to have realized it at the time of his February 12 report, but the British forces withdrawn from the Apalachicola for the attack on New Orleans had returned. Andrew Jackson's spectacular victory at Chalmette on January 8 had forced the British to return to their ships and focus elsewhere. Lt. Col. Nicolls was not back at Prospect Bluff with his Marines and additional troops from a West Indian regiment. News of the appearance of the American agent's force north of the forks prompted an immediate reinforcement of the outpost with additional troops and warriors. That the men of Fowltown were among the warriors defending the fort was made clear by Hawkins' report of February 20:

---

[89] *Ibid.*

...Colo. Nicolls with 200 troops white and black and an assemblage of 500 Warriors is just below the forks. They have an intrenched post picketed, with one Howitzer and one cohorn. The Indians are mostly from the Simenolies of East Florida, and Oketyocanne, Fowl town, and Cheauhau within our limits. They are well supplied with cloths and munitions of War. McQueen and Francis are in Uniform. Every party as they arrive give the War whoop, fire their guns and paint for war. The Indians chastised by Jackson are very humble. The Colo. is gone down today as he says "for his supplies to march towards Charleston, where he soon expects to hear of the arrival of Lord Hill, with a powerful force. He is to set free Negros, compel the Americans to restore back the lands to the Indians, and make every thing submit to him as he marches along. He will bring his cannon up the river with him." He is a great boaster promises any thing and every thing to attach the Indians to his party.[90]

The Royal Navy also moved to assist in the defense of the outpost by sending "eight men in the yawl with a Carronade" up to the forks. A carronade was a short naval cannon that could fire a heavy projectile. William Rawlins, the commander of the HMS *Borer* (the vessel from which the yawl was detached), reported that the American force threating the fort was composed of 50 white cavalry and around 900 Creek warriors.[91]

Hawkins referred to his position about the forks as "112 Mile Camp" or "Camp 112 Mile." It was actually Tocktoethla, the town of Thomas

---

[90] Col. Benjamin Hawkins to Gov. Peter Early, February 20, 1815, Hargrett Rare Book and Manuscript Library, The University of Georgia Libraries, Telamon Cuyler Collection, Box 75, Folder 25, Document 21.
[91] Lt. William Rawlins to Rear Admiral Percy Malcolm, February 26, 1815, Cochrane Papers.

Perryman, which had been evacuated at some point prior to the arrival of the U.S. force on the scene. Fowltown at this time was located directly across the river from Perryman's town and was also found to be abandoned:

> ...I find that Woodbine and his followers are returned to their head quarters below the confluence of the rivers and most probably [all] who were preparing for acts of hostility against your frontiers. We hear only of one or two straggling parties being out. Since the disaster of the British forces at New Orleans the general opinion among them is they will have peace this spring. If a movement should be attempted from where the enemy are we shall have some fighting but I believe the Indians below are under serious apprehensions for their safety. The women and children in the utmost distress for food. All have fled from between the forks. We have found in their houses 50 muskets and 650 musket flints and have heard of more.[92]

Hawkins by now had gone on the defensive and no longer considered an attack on the British fort to be a realistic possibility. The failure of Georgia to send white troops to participate in the campaign was the cause of much concern for his Native American soldiers, especially after they learned that militia soldiers had arrived to garrison the forts where their women and children were awaiting the outcome of the campaign. They convened a council on the night of February 20 and presented their statement to the agent on the next morning:

> We were enrolled in public service by order of General Jackson, promised soldiers pay and rations, and

---

[92] Col. Benjamin Hawkins to Gov. Peter Early, February 24, 1815, Hargrett Rare Book and Manuscript Library, the University of Georgia Libraries, Telamon Cuyler Collection, Box 76, Folder 25, Document 22.

ordered to take care of this frontier. We had selected some of our best men to garrison the posts, we were promised by Colo. Hawkins and General McIntosh a force of white troops to act with us, and while we were out on duty we hear 300 men have taken possession of the posts, our women and children are there and we well know these men are rude and ungovernable. We find we are to have no meat. If white soldiers were with us and would live without it we could and would do it. We hear not of the white force promised us, and why is it these people did not come to help us, and not stop where they have nothing to do?[93]

The situation was deteriorating for the U.S. force. Provisions were running short and the foraging parties sent out by Col. Hawkins were unable to find many cows that they could confiscate for beef. With his Creek soldiers now disgruntled over the failure of more white troops to support them, the agent did his best to hold his command together in the face of an enemy that was growing stronger by the day. It was fortunate for him that the situation soon resolved itself:

Yesterday about one o'clock I received express from Capt. Limbaugh a copy of the despatch from the postmaster genl of 14th announcing the arrival of a treat of peace. I immediately sent off two runners with the information to the British commandant below. They met a flag of truce bringing information to me from their admiral of the same import, Two officers Lieuts. One of the navy and the other of the army bore the flag. They brought the 9th art. Of the treaty only, it being all they had recd. The officers remained with me last evening and returned today. This event yesterday was

---

[93] Statement of Chiefs, February 21, 1815, enclosed in Hawkins to Early, February 20, 1815.

> communicated to ever command who fired a feu de joie, and this morning they paraded in one line as the British officers received with us the line and one other feu de joie was fired.[94]

The firing of even one *feu de joie* was a special and rare event for soldiers of the War of 1812 era. Also called the "rippling fire," the salute was reserved for momentous occasions. It basically consisted of all of the soldiers forming a line and firing in rapid succession, one after another. The result was the appearance of a rippling explosion of fire than ran down the entire length of the line. With nearly 1,000 men at his command, the ones ordered by Hawkins must have been remarkable to witness.

The colonel gave orders for his men to prepare to withdraw and they soon set off on their return up the Chattahoochee River to Fort Mitchell. The War of 1812 was over. While the news was joyous to the white Americans and the British, it must have been received with great concern by the people of Fowltown. Forced to flee from two of their towns in less than two years, they were adrift and unsure of their future.

---

[94] Col. Benjamin Hawkins to Gov. Peter Early, February 26, 1815, Telamon Cuyler Collection, Hargrett Rare Book and Manuscript Library, The University of Georgia Libraries, Box 76, Folder 25, Document 23.

8

PRESSURE GROWS

NEAMATHLA AND HIS WARRIORS were still at Nicolls' Outpost when an important council convened there on March 10, 1815. The purpose was to draft an appeal from the Native Americans for permanent diplomatic status and a mutual defense agreement with Great Britain. Lt. Col. Nicolls believed and so informed the chiefs in his auxiliary force that the 9th article of the Treaty of Ghent required that the United States return to them lands lost during the war. He believed that the British government would not abandon the Creeks and Seminoles and so informed them.

The Nicolls' Outpost Council of 1815 was probably the most significant event in the history of the fort. Neamathla was present, as were two additional chiefs from Fowltown who gave the same name, but were identified by the British as 2nd and 3rd. . Also present were the Prophet Francis, Peter McQueen, Thomas Perryman, William Perryman and more than 30 others. Lt. Col. Nicolls, Capt. Woodbine, Capt. Joseph Roche of the 1st West India Regiment, Capt. Henry Ross of the Rifle Corps and Lt. William Hambly represented the British. The chiefs and warriors were very clear in stating their requests and concerns:

> …We conceive it to be indispensably necessary for our
> good, as well as to make us useful allies of Great Britain,

that British officers should be kept constantly among us, and we request that our good father will grant us this favour. Since Colonel Brown left us, we have been a prey to civil dissensions, fomented and kept up by our inveterate and never-to-be-satisfied foe, the America;s by their bad advice has brother been in the act of shedding the blood of brother: and when the land becomes thus desolated, they possess themselves of it, so that we shall soon be driven to the desert sands of the sea, from the fertile of our forefathers; and we are told that the Spaniards will not let us trade with the British from the mouths of our rivers: we, therefore, further request, that our good father will secure for us the mouths of the rivers Apilachicola, Alabama, and St. Mary's; for, if our communication is once more cut off from his children, we shall be totally ruined.[95]

The chiefs asked that British officers be left among them and reminded King George that by fighting on his behalf they had turned the Americans into even worse enemies:

...[W]e have fought and bled for him against the Americans, by which we have made them our more bitter enemies, and as he has stood the friend of the oppressed nations beyond the great waters, he will surely not forget the sufferings of his once happy children here. We therefore rely on his future protection and his fatherly kindness: we will truly keep the talks which his chief has given us, if he is graciously pleased to continue his protection: famine is now devouring up ourselves and our children, by reason of our Upper Town brethren being driven down upon us in the time the corn was

---

[95] Address of the Indians to the King of England, March 10, 1815, published in the London *Times* on August 13, 1818.

green, and now their miseries and necessities cause them to root up the seed of our future crop, so that we sow in the day we are obliged to watch at night. Was it not for the powder we get from your chief, the whole of the nation would be in dust: the Red Sticks have shot and eat up almost the whole of our cattle, for they have seen their children digging in the woods for want, and who can blame them, when they are pressed by such cruel necessity? Thus are we situated, and are only looking to the departure or the stay of your children, as the signal of our destruction or prosperity.[96]

The chiefs further requested that Lt. Col. Nicolls be appointed as Great Britain's agent to them, objected to the conduct of John Forbes & Company in taking land from them and complained about American encroachments and the building of the Federal Road through the Creek Nation. They also made clear their opinions of William McIntosh:

...McIntosh holds a commission as Major in the American army, and of the Creek Regiment: he has caused much blood to be spilt, for which we denounce him to the whole nation, and will give the usual reward of the brave who may kill him, he having on a recent occasion killed and scalped a brother who was on an errand of peace to our Cherokee brethren, for now other reason alleged against him than his having British arms about him, and in this we are told he has been encouraged by Colonel Hawkins, although long after a peace was declared, and all hostility ordered to cease.[97]

The Prophet Francis was selected by the group to represent their interests to the government in London and he agreed to travel there with

---

[96] *Ibid.*
[97] *Ibid.*

Nicolls when the British evacuated the Apalachicola River. The council ended with a firm expression of willingness by the Seminole, Miccosukee and Perryman faction of the Lower Creeks to establish a permanent relationship with Great Britain. The fort at the forks was evacuated soon after as Nicolls began to consolidate his forces at Prospect Bluff.

Neamathla and his people returned to the vicinity of Perryman's town, probably to their former homes on the west side of the river but then across to the eastern or Georgia side after the death of the elderly Thomas Perryman later that year. Perryman's family and followers moved across the Chattahoochee to Tellmochesses where they joined the town of his son, William. The extensive fields of Tocktoethla were left abandoned and the Fowltown residents soon moved across and occupied them. Their residency there was long remembered by early settlers who called the site "Old Fowltown" for many years before it became known as Fairchild's Landing.

The request of the Native Americans for recognition and assistance from Great Britain was rejected by the government in London. The War of 1812 was over and there was no willingness to reopen it in order to enforce the 9th article of the Treaty of Ghent. The United States believed that the article did not apply to the Creeks because they had signed the separate Treaty of Fort Jackson in August 1814. That agreement was signed almost exclusively by chiefs who had sided with Andrew Jackson during the Creek War of 1813-1814 and no more than one Red Stick was included in the negotiations. Neamathla did not sign nor was he asked to attend the treaty talks. He soon learned, however, that it did not matter. The United States now claimed all of Southwest Georgia.

The only advantage that the Tutalosis could now claim was that they were well supplied with guns and ammunition. In addition to what they had on hand in their village, Nicolls had assured them access to the large arsenal that he left in the magazines of the British Post at Prospect Bluff. This fort was left intact when the British withdrew, still armed with its cannon and housing a massive stockpile of munitions. About one company of the black Colonial Marines opted to stay at the fort with their families instead of evacuating with others to new settlements in Trinidad. They continued to maintain military discipline, hoisted the British flag over the works each day and followed their final orders to prevent the passage of any U.S. or Spanish vessels past the fort. They believed that Nicolls would return as the British agent to the Creeks and Seminoles and had no way of knowing that this request was ultimately rejected by officials in London. American authorities named their settlement the "Negro Fort" and objected to Spanish officials in Pensacola about its existence.

Just one year after they signed the useless request for a continued alliance with the British, the Fowltown chiefs were stunned to learn of the arrival of U.S. soldiers at the mouth of Cemochechobee Creek. Maj. Gen. Edmund P. Gaines had led Lt. Col. Duncan L. Clinch's battalion from the 4th U.S. Infantry down the river from Fort Mitchell to that point for the purpose of building a new fort. The post was named Fort Gaines, after the general, and marked the first effort by the United States to enforce the terms of the Treaty of Fort Jackson on the Native Americans living in Southwest Georgia and Southeast Alabama.[98]

The building of the fort provoked almost universal outrage among the Lower Creeks. The Big Warrior and Little Prince, both of whom had sided with the United States in the Creek War and War of 1812, appeared in person to lodge formal protests:

> In the vicinity of this place I had the opportunity of seeing the Indians in council, where the Big Warrior and Little Prince were both present. You no doubt will recollect that the Big Warrior was friendly to us during the late war. Let me tell you he does not conceal is disapprobation to our running the boundary line. However he received us courteously – not so the Little

---

[98] See Dale Cox and Rachael Conrad, *Fort Gaines, Georgia: A Militiary History*, Bascom, Florida, 2016, for a detailed history of this post.

Prince, who showed us no mark of attention. The Big Warrior is the largest Indian known to us. He is dignified in his demeanor, affable and inviting in his manners; his enemies accuse him of cowardice, but I presume his inactivity of late years is to be ascribed to old age and an unwieldy person. The countenance of the Little Prince indicates him to be fierce and cruel, and I am told it does not belie him. It is perhaps well for the United States, that he is now old and bigoted.[99]

Gen. Gaines used the council to inform the gathered Native Americans that he had come to enforce the peace and survey the new boundary that would divide the Creek Nation from the lands ceded to the United States. He told them that he brought the "pipe of peace" for friends but the "cannon & bayonet" for enemies. "They replied that they were too poor and too weak to oppose us," he continued, "and therefore had determined to sit still and hold down their heads."[100]

The Little Prince held down his head in terms of violence but continued to verbally oppose the building of Fort Gaines. He delivered another talk there on April 26, 1816:

> Jackson and Hawkins spoke to us, and told us we were their children. At the Tuskeegee meeting you told us you would have the land as far down as the Summochichoba; but we chiefs did not agree to it. You did not tell us then you would build forts along the river bank down to the fork; but we heard, since, you issued orders to that effect. We do not think it friendly for one friend to take any thing from another forcibly. The commander and Hawkins did not tell us any thing about building these forts. We hear of your meeting at Tuskeegee. We hope you will detain the forces they are

---

[99] Officer at Fort Gaines to a gentleman in Raleigh, North Carolina, April 16, 1816, published in the *Salem Gazette*, May 21, 1816.
[100] Maj. Gen. Edmund P. Gaines to Maj. Gen. Andrew Jackson, April 18, 1816, Andrew Jackson Papers, 1775-1874, Library of Congress.

at present, and wait on the Indians, as I am sure they will
be able to settle every thing; but all the chiefs are not yet
met. You know that we are slow in our movements.[101]

The Little Prince then went down the Chattahoochee to visit the
Seminoles, Miccosukees, Red Sticks and Lower Creeks below Fort
Gaines to repeat to them his plea that everyone cease their movements
and remain calm until the principal chiefs could meet to discuss the
matter. It did not go well:

> …The Little Prince, and all the chiefs of the friendly
> party, have been below endeavoring to make friends of
> the hostile party, but without effect; the night before last
> a chief of the Seminoles made his appearance at the
> council house with 200 warriors, and dissolved their
> meeting, firing and threatening to put the friendly chiefs
> to death if they did not leave there immediately; some of
> the friendly chiefs passed here to-day on their way
> home.[102]

The identity of the "chief of the Seminoles" who appeared and
violently ended the downriver council was not given in documents of the
time but he may have been Neamathla. Military officers definitely
blamed the warriors of Fowltown for two attacks near Fort Gaines during
the first week of May 1816:

> …Four days since; some of our waggons that were
> returning to Fort Hawkins, were stopped by a small party
> of Indians, only two miles from our camp, and were
> about to be plundered of their horses and no doubt
> scalped, when one of them made his escape to camp, and
> gave us the information. I immediately volunteered with

---

[101] Talk of the Little Prince (Translated by William Hambly), April 26, 1816,
American State Papers – Foreign Affairs, Volume IV: 558.
[102] Officer at Fort Gaines to the Editors of the *Baltimore Patriot*, May 5, 1816,
republished by the *American Beacon* on June 10, 1816.

30 brave men of the 4th regiment, and rescued them, and proceeded 40 miles with them through some hostile towns without further molestation; but during my absence, the same party was guilty of one of the most daring outrages I ever heard of; while two men, belonging to my company, were attending 30 cattle belonging to us, within half a mile of camp, about 12 o'clock, at noon, they were driven off along with two public horses; we sent a small party in pursuit, but without coming up with them; they took the road on to St. Marks, crossing Flint river about 20 miles from its mouth.[103]

Lt. Col. Clinch and other officers at Fort Gaines initially speculated that the attacks might have been carried out by either Seminoles from Florida or some of Peter McQueen's Red Sticks, but subsequent intelligence placed the blame on the Tutalosis. The bold raid left no doubt of the degree to which the lower towns opposed the taking of their lands. War now appeared to be imminent and an anonymous officer informed the editors of the *Baltimore Patriot* that the garrison expected to be attacked at any minute:

...Today we heard of 250 of the lower warriors being about 40 miles from here; so that you may expect to hear of some scalping in this quarter very soon; our force is very inconsiderable, not 300 effective men. I have the command of a fine company, and three good field pieces, 2 six pounders and a 4; and I hope that you will hear a good account of us should we be attacked, I wish to see more Indian fighting.[104]

Lt. Col. Clinch provided more information in a report to Maj. Gen. Gaines on May 7, 1816. A spy sent on the trail of the raiding party had followed them as far as the present-day site of Bainbridge, Georgia:

---

[103] *Ibid.*
[104] *Ibid.*

...The Spy I sent over the Flint, returned on the 5th instant, and informed me that he learnt that the party that took the soldiers and cattle, came from the Flint, that they crossed that river at Burges's old place, and that they had not killed the men at that time, but he understood they intended doing so if they become too much fatigued to travel to the Negro Fort where they intended carrying them. He further states that he understood from some of his friends in that quarter, that the Semilones, all the Towns on the Flint near the Confluence of the two rivers, and most of those on the Chattohoochee were preparing for war – that they had been dancing and drinking their war Physic for several days that they had determined to divide themselves into two parties, one party to go against Hartford (Georgia) and the other to come up and attack the Troops under my Command.[105]

The Native Americans along the border were well supplied with arms and ammunition from the Fort at Prospect Bluff ("Negro Fort") and had the benefit of that post as a defensive citadel should they be defeated and forced to fall back. They did not know that the United States also had its eyes on the fort. Gaines and Clinch were in the final stages of readying a campaign against Prospect Bluff. Not only would the soldiers not remain quietly at Fort Gaines in accordance with the request of the Little Prince, they would soon move all the way down the Chattahoochee its confluence with the Flint where they would build yet another fort. Supply ships would be sent via the Gulf of Mexico with an armed escort from U.S. Navy gunboats. Should any opposition be encountered at the bluff, Clinch was authorized to destroy the "Negro Fort."[106]

---

[105] Lt. Col. Duncan L. Clinch to Maj. Gen. Edmund P. Gaines, May 7, 1816, Jackson Papers, Library of Congress.
[106] Maj. Gen. Edmund P. Gaines to Commodore Daniel Patterson, May 22, 1816, *American State Papers – Foreign Affairs*, Volume IV: 559.

Clinch and Gaines by now were especially wary of Neamathla, who they came to believe was a key leader in the opposition to the presence of U.S. troops on the lower Chattahoochee. Fowltown was one of the villages that Clinch had in mind when he outlined the planned scope of his initial operations to Gaines on May 9, 1816:

> ...I am extremely anxious to move down on those fellows, and will do so as soon as the state of my provisions and ammunition will admit of it. I propose ordering two companies of the Battalion of the 4th now on their march from Charleston, to leave their heavy baggage at the Agency and join me as soon as possible. I then propose leaving all my heavy baggage, and a sufficient number of men to man the boats at this post, and move the balance of my command down the river by rapid marches, and destroy every hostile town between this and the Confluence of the two rivers, after which my boats can drop down with ease and safety in two days. I will then select a strong position on the Flint, fortify my Camp, move up that river, and destroy all the Towns to Burgess old place, and order the Command left at the Agency to descend the Flint with our supplies, and if my force will admit of it; I will pursue the enemy further, and strike a blow in another quarter.[107]

The Little Prince had attempted to convince the lower towns to remain at peace with the whites and join forces instead for an attack on Prospect Bluff. They had no interest in such a move because they considered the maroons living there to be allies and because many of the arms and munitions stored in the fort had been left for their use. Instead, as Clinch detailed, they focused their ire instead on the Prince and the U.S. Army:

---

[107] Lt. Col. Duncan L. Clinch to Maj. Gen. Edmund P. Gaines, May 9, 1816, Jackson Papers, Library of Congress.

The Prince told me that he had done everything that lay in his power, to induce the lower Indians to go against the Negro Fort, and to let the white people alone, but that they were crazy, and would not listen to him – That they had deceived him for some time, but that at last he had discovered they were determined on their own distruction, and that I might do as I pleased with them. From what I can learn of Hambly, it appears that himself, the Prince and party, had to run off and that a party of the Tuttoloses pursued them, with the intention (if taken) to keep the Prince a prisoner, and to burn himself. He further states it as his opinion, that they cannot raise more than 500 men, that will go to war. The Tuttolosees and Miccosookus, are the principal instigators, but he thinks most of the Towns on the Flint, below Barnetts, and several towns on the East Bank of the Chattohoochie will join them.[108]

The report by Clinch left no doubt that the warriors of Fowltown and Miccosukee were prepared to go to war against the United States. The Little Prince's estimate that they could not raise more than 500 men was true only in regard to those two towns. They would be supported in the event of war by the Red Sticks from the bands of Francis, McQueen and others as well as by many other Lower Creek and Seminole warriors. The British had expected to field more than 3,500 warriors in their planned campaign against Georgia and the number prepared to support Neamathla and Cappachimico was probably similar.

It now came down to a matter of which force would move first.

---

[108] *Ibid.*

9

TENSION ON THE FRONTIER

THE CONFRONTATION BETWEEN NEAMATHLA and Lt. Col. Duncan Lamont Clinch began with the Tutalosi raids at Fort Gaines in May 1816 and would continue for the next two years. The United States regarded the events that followed as a series of confrontations while the warriors of Fowltown clearly believed that a state of war existed between them and the whites.

As the two leaders faced off on the lower Chattahoochee River, many of the towns along the stretch of river that divided them just wanted to get out of the way:

> …Several of the chiefs below and near me have come in and begged protection, they state that they have their crops in the ground, and unless I will let them stay at home and till them, their women and children must starve. I have told them to stay at home and make their corn, that when I approached their towns, the Chiefs must meet me with their warriors without arms, that I would take a list of them, and if any of them joined the hostile party, they were never to suffer them to return again, on pain on having their towns destroyed. This they willingly agreed to and the Prince informed me that

he had ordered all the Chiefs that wish to remain friendly, to come and see me as soon as possible.[109]

Any chiefs that came to see Clinch were told to make their crops, harvest their corn and then to move from their longtime homes to new locations above the boundary of the now reduced in size Creek Nation. Fort Gaines marked the new limits. Everything south of the post now belonged to the United States per the Treaty of Fort Jackson and to remain at peace with the whites, the Native Americans living in this vast region must pack up and leave.

Neamathla had no intention of following these orders. He had not signed the Treaty of Fort Jackson and, as he would later express, did not consider it as binding on him. The Fowltown people were still living on the east side of the Chattahoochee at Perryman's old town, a site that offered good water, open fields and access to the rich hunting lands around the forks of the Chattahoochee and Flint. They were rebuilding their lives and were prepared to fight in order to stay in a place that they liked.

Anticipating that widespread combat could erupt at any moment, Neamathla and some of his principal warriors left Fowltown in late May and went down to Prospect Bluff. Their intent was to bring back a large stock of arms and ammunition so they would be prepared for the fighting that they expected to come. Lt. Col. Clinch, however, received his orders from Maj. Gen. Gaines at the same time and immediately began his move down the Chattahoochee River. He approached Fowltown before the chief and his warriors could return:

> ...Our movements were so rapid the Indians had no knowledge of our being on the river until they saw our boats as soon as we approached Fowl Town. The Cowardly rascals hoisted a white flag and appeared to be

---

[109] Lt. Col. Duncan L. Clinch to Maj. Gen. Edmund P. Gaines, May 9, 1816, Jackson Papers, Library of Congress.

much alarmed. I [invited] their chief on board, but was informed by the Indian that came on board that he had not returned from the N.F. [i.e. Negro Fort] where he had been for the purpose of procuring ammunition. I learnt last evening that he has since returned and have ordered him to be here in two days & shall be governed in my future operations by circumstances.[110]

The story likely would have been very different had Neamathla and all of his warriors been present when the military boats approached. Their absence, however, allowed Clinch to continue past Fowltown to the forks. Unable to find a suitable site there for the construction of a fort, he turned up the Flint River and finally settled on a commanding red clay bluff on the left bank of that stream. The soldiers began work on a new fort there, a temporary work that the named Camp Crawford in honor of Secretary of War William Crawford of Georgia. It is better known by its later name – Fort Scott.

Once he felt secure within the log walls of the new stockade, Clinch sent preemptory orders to Neamathla requiring the chief to appear before him:

> …I had ordered Ene emartler to come in to see me in two days. In answer to my first order he sent me word that he was very anxious to see me but that he was very busy with his corn and could not come for some time. I immediately sent a friendly chief called Yellow Hair, to inform him that unless he came down immediately I would send for him and have him taken and would treat him and his town as enemies. On receiving my last order he consented to come down, but manifested a great deal of fear & apprehension.[111]

---

[110] Lt. Col. Duncan L. Clinch to Maj. Gen. Edmund P. Gaines, June 12, 1816, Jackson Papers, Library of Congress.

Yellow Hair, a chief from Tamathli in present-day Jackson County, Florida, had sided with the British during the War of 1812. They were gone now so he had cast his lot with the United States. Clinch's information on Neamathla's response to his demands likely came from Yellow Hair. The description might well have been accurate, but if so it was counter to every other known account of the Fowltown chief:

> ...On arriving on the opposite side of the river his heart failed him and he told the chief that he could not come into the fort (as he called it) but wished me to cross over and see him. I directed the Adjutant to go over with the Interpreter and Chief and to tell him that unless he came over immediately that he had orders to compel him to come on which he came over and I never saw a poor devil manifest as much fear as he did. I had several friendly chiefs with me and they all informed me that they never saw him so completely cut down before. He consented to every demand I made of him and informed me that King Hago would come and see me in a short time and that everything should be settled as I wished it.[112]

Clinch's treatment of Neamathla would have been humiliating to him or any other chief and may have contributed significantly to the lingering bitterness that he felt for the U.S. Army in particular and whites in general. The silence that the officer took as fear was probably simply the chief's way of dealing with an uncomfortable situation that was beyond his control. His mention of "King Hago" was a reference to Cappachimico, the head chief of Miccosukee. Neamathla's promise that the powerful Miccosukee leader would soon arrive and "everything

---

[111] Lt. Col. Duncan L. Clinch to Maj. Gen. Edmund P. Gaines, June 14, 1816, Jackson Papers, Library of Congress.
[112] *Ibid.*

should be settled" may have had more meaning than the lieutenant colonel realized.

Lt. Col. Clinch left Camp Crawford with 112 men in boats on July 10, 1816. He joined forces with a large party of Cowetas and other pro-U.S. Creeks as he made his way down the Apalachicola River and soon surrounded the "Negro Fort" at Prospect Bluff, cutting off all escape for the 320 or so men, women and children sheltered behind its walls. Garcon, the commander of the fort, responded to a demand for surrender with a cannon shot and raised the Union Jack and a red flag of no surrender over the ramparts. The troops and Creeks battled the occupants of the fort for seven days before a heated cannonball from U.S. Gunboat No. 154 set a fire that spread through an open door and exploded the primary magazine on the morning of July 27. The explosion was so large that the ground could be felt to shake as far away as Pensacola. It was undoubtedly felt by Neamathla and the people of Fowltown. U.S. officers estimated that 270 of the 320 people in the fort were killed instantly. Most of the remaining 50 were badly injured and many died over the next few days. U.S. troops and their Creek allies confiscated a massive stockpile of cannon, arms, ammunition and military supplies.[113]

Garcon had managed to get couriers out before the fort was completely surrounded and one or more of these reached both Fowltown and Miccosukee. The chiefs and warriors immediately took up the line of march, intending to break the siege and join in the defense of the fort:

> On the evening of the first inst. I received information that a large body of Seminole Indians were within a day's march of us, and in a few hours the report was confirmed by a letter from Major Cutler left in command at Camp Crawford informing me that a large body of Seminoles were descending the Appalachicola. I immediately ordered Major Muhlenburgh to keep the

---

[113] See Dale Cox, *The Fort at Prospect Bluff*, scheduled for release in early 2018.

boats together, and to be in readiness to receive them, and directed one hundred Indians to keep with the Boats, and to act in concert if necessary. I advanced with two hundred Cowetas under the gallant Major McIntosh to meet them, but the cowardly wretches dispersed without our being able to get a view of them.[114]

The explosion of the "Negro Fort" exceeded anything that anyone had ever seen before. Clinch and other army officers wrote of how they shed tears at the sight of so many bodies and parts of bodies scattered across the bluff. Unsure of how the military had achieved such destruction, the Native American relief force withdrew instead of fighting. The United States believed that the blast had so intimidated the Creeks, Miccosukees and Seminoles that they would stay peaceful and quiet for the foreseeable future.

Neamathla's first action following the disaster was to instruct the people of Fowltown to pack their belongings. The village on the Chattahoochee lay between two U.S. forts and was exposed to the regular passage of military boats. It would be necessary for the Tutalosis to relocate once again.

The new site for Fowltown was Four Mile Creek, a swampy stream that flows into the Flint River about four miles south of present-day Bainbridge. The Lower Creek town of Oklafunee had stood at the mouth of the creek during the American Revolution but was abandoned in the years that followed. Its old fields were fallow and overgrown, but would be easier to clear and farm than the old growth forests that surrounded them. The swamp offered not just food, but a place of safety and security in the event of an attack. The higher ridges and hills that ringed what is today known as Fowltown Swamp were covered with wiregrass and longleaf pine and provided good grazing areas for free-roaming livestock.

---

[114] Lt. Col. Duncan L. Clinch to Col. Robert Butler, August 2, 1816, Jackson Papers, Library of Congress.

The Tutalosi villagers reestablished themselves on the south side of the creek during the late summer and fall of 1816. They built cabins, corncribs and other structures there and stocked away as much of their corn crop from the "Old Fowltown" site on the Chattahoochee River as possible. The new village site was also much closer to Miccosukee and Tallahassee Talofa. These large villages could help with food for the winter and were also connected to the new site by direct roads which would allow quick reinforcement by hundreds of warriors in the event of an attack.

Camp Crawford, meanwhile, became Fort Scott in early fall, the new name signifying the intention of the army to occupy the post on a long-term basis. Construction was started on permanent facilities that included barracks, officers' quarters and a larger stockade. It soon became apparent to Lt. Col. Clinch that the destruction of the Fort at Prospect Bluff had failed to shock the chiefs and warriors of the vicinity into submission. When cost-cutting orders arrived from Washington, D.C., requiring him to leave a detachment at Fort Scott and then evacuate the rest of his battalion from there at Fort Gaines, Clinch assumed the responsibility for countermanding the directive. He instead abandoned Fort Scott at the end of December 1816 but left a sufficient force at Fort Gaines to protect that post and fend off an attack. George Perryman, a son of the late Thomas Perryman, was employed as caretaker for the post and the supplies being left there.

Neamathla and other chiefs in the area soon heard that the troops had departed and by late January 1817 they appeared at the gates of Fort Scott:

> Perryman states in his letter that the Red Sticks, (or hostiles) after we had left the fort, came in companies and carried off every thing we had left with him, and what he had purchased of Butler; burnt three houses, and threatened, if he did not leave the place, to burn it over his head. He got what few articles he could, with his

family, in a canoe, and came to his brother's, who informs me that there are at present about 300 Indians embodied at the forks, and others constantly joining them. He does not know their intentions, but understood a party was going out to steal horses &c. &c.[115]

The burning of Fort Scott was a remarkably bold move by the Tutalosi and other warriors. It was the first step in a northward surge that took them to the gates of Fort Gaines and beyond. Settlers in the vicinity of the latter post were confronted and told to leave. George Perryman, meanwhile, soon sent a personal letter up to Fort Gaines with intelligence on the activities of both Fowltown, which he described as the "lower town on Flint," and the Alachua and Black Seminoles in Florida:

...There was a friend of mine not long since in the lower town on Flint & he saw many horses, cattle and hoggs that had came immediately from the State of Georgia and they are bringing them away continually, they speak in the most contemptuous manner of the Americans and threaten to have satisfaction for what has been done meaning the Destruction of the neagro fort, there is another of my acquaintances returned immediately from the Seminolie Towns, and saw the neagroes there on parade. He counted about Six Hundred that bore arms, they have chosen officers of every description and indeavour to keep up a Regular Disciplin and is Very strict in punishing violators of their Military orders. There is said to be about the same number of Indians belonging to their party & there is of Both neagroes & Indians daily going to their standard, they say they are in complete fit for fighting and wishes an Engagement with the Americans or McIntosh's Troops, they would let

---

[115] Lt. Richard M. Sands to the Commanding Officer at Fort Hawkins, February 2, 1817, Jackson Papers, Library of Congress.

them know they had something more to do than they had at Appalachiciola. They have Chosen Bolegs for their head and nominated him king and pays him all kind of Monarchial Respect almost to Idolatry, keeping a picket guard at the distance of five miles.[116]

The chief that Perryman called "Bolegs" or "Bowlegs" was called Boleck by the Spanish. He had been forced to relocate from the Paynes Prairie region to the west side of the Suwannee River after Tennessee militia invaded Florida and attacked the Alachua during the so-called Patriot War of 1812-1813. Whether the information received by Perryman that Boleck had been named "king" of the Seminoles was accurate is not clear. He does need seem to have exercised such control during the coming First Seminole War. The claim by another informant that numerous stolen horses, cows and hogs had been seen at Fowltown was probably accurate.

In a curious statement, Perryman went on to report that the Miccosukee chief, Cappachimico, was opposed to war with the United States. This represents a major change in view for him but the departure of the British at the end of the War of 1812 and the destruction of the "Negro Fort" may have discouraged him.[117]

The situation on the border grew dramatically worse in February 1817 when a party of warriors attacked the Garrett home near the Okefenokee Swamp in Georgia:

> On the 24th instant the house of Mr. Garrett, residing in the upper part of this county, near the boundary of Wayne Co. was attacked, during his absence near the middle of the day, by this party consisting of about fifteen, who shot Mrs. Garrett in two

---

[116] George Perryman to Lt. Richard M. Sands, February 24, 1817, Jackson Papers, Library of Congress.
[117] *Ibid.*

places, and then dispatched her by stabbing and scalping. Her two children, one about three years & the other two months, were also murdered, and the eldest scalped; the house was then plundered of every article of value, and set on fire – a young man in the neighbourhood at work hearing the report of guns went immediately towards the house were he discovered the murdered family. The flames having only commenced were soon extinguished – and he spread the alarm.[118]

The warriors were trailed by local volunteers but escaped by crossing back into Spanish Florida via a trail that led to the Suwannee River and Miccosukee. William Perryman, brother of George, soon arrived at Fort Gaines with information that the anti-U.S. forces were being led by Peter McQueen and that a woman and two children had recently been killed by them. Maj. Gen. Jackson urged the settlement of the treaty lands to separate the Creeks from the Red Sticks, Miccosukees and Seminoles in Florida. Maj. Gen. Gaines was more pragmatic. He ordered a company of artillery from Charleston Harbor to reoccupy and repair Fort Scott and instructed the army's contractors to move a large number of rations to the frontier:

> You are hereby required to keep up a supply of rations for one hundred men at Fort Scott near the confluence of Flint and Chatahoochie rivers, for Four Months always in advance. This supply to consist of Flour and Bacon or such Pickled Pork as may have been preserved for safe keeping through the summer, together with the small parts of the ration required by the contract – the whole to be kept in store, independent of the casual supplies of fresh beef &c., depending upon the thing settlements in the vicinity of that post. The above supply

---

[118] Archibald Clark to Maj. Gen. Edmund P. Gaines, February 26, 1817, Jackson Papers, Library of Congress.

for the first four months maybe deposited and issued at Fort Gaines, until ordered by the Commanding Officer at that Post to Fort Scott.[119]

Tensions grew even more when a letter reached Fort Gaines from a new player. An elderly trader named Alexander Arbuthnot had arrived in Florida from the Bahamas with hopes of supplanting the trade monopoly of John Forbes & Company. He met with the Red Sticks, Seminoles and Miccosukees and soon began to represent them – "unofficially" he claimed – in their dealings with U.S. authorities. In March, for example, he filed a claim on behalf of Peter McQueen asking that the United States return slaves lost to him during the Creek War.[120]

The United States immediately branded Arbuthnot as a British agent and expressed considerable alarm about his presence in Florida. Capt. Sanders Donoho left Charleston with a company from the 4th U.S. Artillery on April 27, 1817. It would take him until June to reach Fort Scott and even longer to get the burned fort into a defensible condition. A second artillery unit was sent to the St. Marys. Units of U.S. Infantry would soon follow.[121]

Allegations, meanwhile, flew back and forth between the Native Americans and whites during the spring of 1817. Another party of warriors drove off a herd of cattle from above the St. Marys River, prompting the Georgia militia to invade Florida. The soldiers attacked two small groups of either Seminole or Miccosukee warriors but may have attacked the wrong people. David B. Mitchell, the former governor of Georgia, had just accepted the appointment to replace Col. Benjamin Hawkins as the U.S. Agent for Indian Affairs. Hawkins had died a short time before. Mitchell, however, resumed the veteran agent's work quickly and soon reported that the militia had actually attacked a party of

---

[119] Maj. Gen. Edmund P. Gaines to the Contractor for the State of Georgia, March 24, 1817, Jackson Papers, Library of Congress.
[120] Alexander Arbuthnot to the Officer Commanding at Fort Gaines, March 3, 1817, Jackson Papers, Library of Congress.
[121] Report from Charleston, S.C., April 28, 1817, published in the *Georgia Journal* on May 6, 1817.

Osoochee warriors from the lower Chattahoochee River. They had not been involved in the cattle raids, he reported.[122]

Through it all, Neamathla and the people of Fowltown worked to build their new community on Four Mile Creek. The U.S. Army had retreated from Fort Scott and the Tutalosis had helped to burn the hated fort to the ground. They hoped to return to their normal lives now that the soldiers were gone and despite the whirlwind swirling around them, fostered hopes of a peaceful existence in the swamps and hills of present-day Decatur County, Georgia.

---

[122] David B. Mitchell to the Acting Governor of Georgia, June 10, 1817, published in the *Georgia Journal* on June 24, 1817.

10

"THE POWERS ABOVE"

THE REOCCUPATION OF FORT SCOTT by U.S. troops in June 1817 was unexpected and outrageous in the view of Neamathla. Capt. Sanders Donoho reached the post from Charleston in mid-June and was reinforced about one month later by Brevet Maj. David E. Twiggs and his company from the 7th U.S. Infantry. Twiggs came overland from Fort Crawford at present-day East Brewton, Alabama, while his company's heavy supplies were sent by water from Mobile with an escort under 1st Lt. Richard W. Scott. The overland force built a new road from Fort Crawford to Fort Gaines, stopping along the way to throw up blockhouses at key river crossings.

The return of the troops to Fort Scott was watched carefully by the chiefs of the area and not all of them were unhappy to see the soldiers. William Perryman, for example, was bitter over the abuses that his brother had suffered when the post was burned by Tutalosis and Red Sticks earlier in the year. He welcomed the return of the army and appeared outside the gates of the fort soon after the arrival there of Bvt. Maj. Twiggs. Perryman requested that the major convene a council so area chiefs could speak in a show of support for the United States. Twiggs agreed and the meeting was set for August 4.

At some point either before or shortly after the council, Maj. Twiggs learned that Perryman had another object in mind:

...The objects of the chiefs and warriors who attended that meeting, was, to have a talk with the commanding officer, (myself,) for the purpose of expressing their friendship for the United States, and their intention of remaining at peace with the United States. I understood, from another source, which at the time, I deemed to be conclusive evidence of the fact, that one object of the chiefs and warriors who attended the meeting, had in view, was to flog, in my presence, the chief of the Fowl Town, Eneheemathla, for his permitting his warriors to commit depredations on the inhabitants of the Georgia frontier, and afterwards stating those outrages, committed by his own people, to have been committed by the people of their own towns.[123]

It is impossible to imagine the result that a public flogging of Neamathla might have sparked, but William Perryman was not alone in his desire to punish the Fowltown chief. The council also attracted the first and second chiefs of Ekanachatte, Ocheesee Talofa and Choconicla. All three of these towns supported the British during the War of 1812, as did the Perryman towns.

It is interesting to note that all four of the towns represented at the meeting were located on the west bank of the Chattahoochee and Apalachicola Rivers in Spanish Florida. This placed them outside of the jurisdiction of the United States. Ekanachatte, Tellmochesses and Choconicla (formerly Tamathli) were in what is now Jackson County, Florida, while Ocheesee Talofa was at the bluff of that name in Calhoun County. Their plan to flog a Lower Creek chief at a U.S. military post was problematic from a legal standpoint but Neamathla was not in a position to seek redress in the courts.

------

[123] Maj. David E. Twiggs to Lt. Daniel Burch, Aide-de-Camp for Lt. Col. Matthew Arbuckle, October 7, 1819, Reports of Committees: 16th Congress, 1st Session – 49th Congress, 1st session, Library of Congress.

The chief was a smart man, however, and knew that no good could come from his appearance for a council at Fort Scott:

> ...The talk was delayed until nearly 4 o'clock in the evening, waiting for the Fowl Town chief, Eneheemathla and his warriors. I did not see or hear from either that chief or his warriors, during that day, nor until several days afterwards. He was duly notified of the meeting, in a message sent by myself. This meeting of the chiefs and warriors was called by myself, at the particular request of William Perryman, chief in the lower towns, or those on the Chatahouchie, below the Indian boundary line.[124]

With Perryman's plan to flog the Fowltown chief now dashed, the other chiefs went forward with the talks. In addition to William Perryman, they included Econchattimico from Ekanachatte, John Yellow Hair from Choconicla and Jack Mealy of Ocheesee Talofa. The second chiefs and other head men of all four towns were also present. They told Maj. Twiggs of their wish to live at peace with the United States but expressed their doubts that the towns east of the Flint and Apalachicola Rivers were so inclined.[125]

They were correct about Fowltown and the other villages east of the rivers. Maj. Gen. Edmund P. Gaines planned to demand that Miccosukee surrender the warriors responsible for the attacks on the St. Marys River. Bvt. Maj. Twiggs warned, however, that he did not expect that they would be surrendered to the whites. He also warned that Neamathla had made his position emphatically clear:

> I have not heard a word from the Seminolas that can be relied on, but in my opinion they will never give up a murderer to the whites. In fact the Chief of Fowl town

---

[124] *Ibid.*
[125] *Ibid.*

near this who is very frequently among the Seminolas told me eight days ago that the Flint river was the line between us & I must not cut another stick of timber on the opposite side from this, the land was his & he was directed by the Powers above to protect & defend it & he should do so & I would see that talking could not frighten him since which I have not seen one of his town. The Indians on the east of the Flint will in my opinion in the event of a movement on that side of the river commence hostilities. It is possible I may be mistaken but I shall think so till the contrary is proved.[126]

Twiggs' report was dated August 11, 1817, seven days after the council at Fort Scott. This means that his conversation with Neamathla must have taken place on August 3, the day before that meeting. He later explained that the chief had outlined his position on U.S. demands that he evacuate the lands ceded by the Treaty of Fort Jackson:

…Eneheemauthla, the chief of Fowl Town, stated to me, previous to the arrival of the troops under general Gaines at Fort Scott, in November, 1817, that he had nothing to do with giving the land away at Fort Jackson, (as he called it,) and that he should not consider that act as binding on him or his people, nor would they remove in consequence, unless compelled by force; that he supposed the Indians on the Chattahouchie had fooled away their land, but that the land on his side of the Flint River (the left bank) belonged to him and his people, and that he should defend it, saying he was directed to do so by the Powers above. He intimated to me, in plain terms, that if ever a detachment of United States troops crossed the Flint River he would resist them by force. He also

---

[126] Bvt. Maj. David E. Twiggs to Maj. Gen. Edmund P. Gaines, August 11, 1817, Jackson Papers, Library of Congress.

cautioned me not to turn over there either horses or cattle, nor to get timber from off the land, as he was determined it should not be done except by force.[127]

Neamathla's actual words to Twiggs were subjected to a bit of spin by later in the fall. He had told the major that he was "directed by the powers above" to defend his land and would do so. Maj. Gen. Gaines later adapted the quote to read that the chief had been "directed by the powers above and below." The implication was clear.[128]

The exchange of words between the chief and Maj. Twiggs was also reported by Edmund Doyle, the storekeeper for the John Forbes & Company trading post at Prospect Bluff. The store had been reestablished following the destruction of the "Negro Fort" and Doyle reported rumors of Neamathla's comments soon after they were made:

> …[Half] of the 250,000 rations required by Genl Gaines are partly here and partly on their route to Forts Scott and Gaines on these waters – [Cappachimico's] last message to the Commandant at Fort Scott Flint River was rather insulting – he said he had no talks for him – that he expected shortly an English agent who would settle the affairs of the Indians, and drive the Americans back – another fellow the Fowl Town Chief ordered them not to cut trees on the east of Flint river – and is otherwise high crested they have also refused to give an audience to one of the officers sent to them by General Gaines – all these circumstances will hasten on the remainder of the provisions and as soon as they are in deposit an overwhelming force enters the Nation which settles their affairs shortly.[129]

---

[127] Twiggs to Burch, October 7, 1819.
[128] Maj. Gen. Edmund P. Gaines to the Governor of Georgia, November 21, 1817, published in the *American Advocate*, December 27, 1817.

Gen. Gaines had reached the same conclusion but decided to make one final demand that the warriors responsible for attacks on whites be surrendered to the army. An interpreter named Gregory carried his written ultimatum to Miccosukee on September 6, 1817, where it was read and explained to a gathering of the town's chiefs and warriors. Gregory was protected while in Miccosukee but reported to Maj. Twiggs that the situation there had been tense:

> The interpreter informed me that the principal warriors were not present when he was there, but those who were present said they had never heard of Indians being given up to be punished by the whites; that they had heard of their being sometimes killed by themselves for offences committed, but seemed to think that giving them up was out of the question, but said they would have a meeting, and would answer the letter in a few days. As they have not done so, I think but one construction can be put on their conduct. The young men seemed to dislike the communication very much, and when Gregory was about leaving the town he offered his hand to an Indian, who held out his with a knife in it, and refused to shake hands with him; he staid so short a time among them that it was impossible for him to give much information respecting them.[130]

Cappachimico promised a reply within ten days but seems to have misunderstood that he should send it to Fort Scott. Twiggs expected to receive there and found its failure to arrive in a timely fashion to be sinister. The chief's response, however, was delivered instead to Fort

---

[129] Edmund Doyle to James Innerarity, August 17, 1817, published in the *Alexandria Gazette*, October 24, 1817.
[130] Bvt. Maj. David E. Twiggs to Maj. Gen. Edmund P. Gaines, September 17, 1817, *American State Papers – Indian Affairs*, Volume I, page 158.

Hawkins at present-day Macon, Georgia. It was undoubtedly reduced to writing by Alexander Arbuthnot and may reflect some of his thinking as well as or in the place of some of Cappachimico's. Either way, it made very clear the position of the Miccosukees:

> Since the last war, after you sent word we must quit the war, we, the red people, have come over to this side. The white people have carried all the red people's cattle off. After the war I sent to all my people to let the white people along, and stay on this side of the river, and they did so; but the white people still continue to carry off their cattle. Barnard's son was here, and I inquired of him what was to be done, and he said we must go to the headman of the white people and complain. I did so, and there was no white headman, and there was no law in this case. The whites first began, and there is nothing said about that, but great complaint made about what the Indians do. This is now three years since the white people killed three Indians; since that they have killed three other Indians, and taken their horses and what they had; and this summer they killed three more, and very lately they killed one more. We sent word to the white people that these murders were done, and the answer was that they were people that were outlaws, and we ought to go and kill them. The white people killed our people first, and the Indians then took satisfaction.[131]

---

[131] Kenhajo (i.e. Cappachimico) to the Commanding Officer at Fort Hawkins, September 18, 1817, *American State Papers – Indian Affairs*, Volume I, page 159.

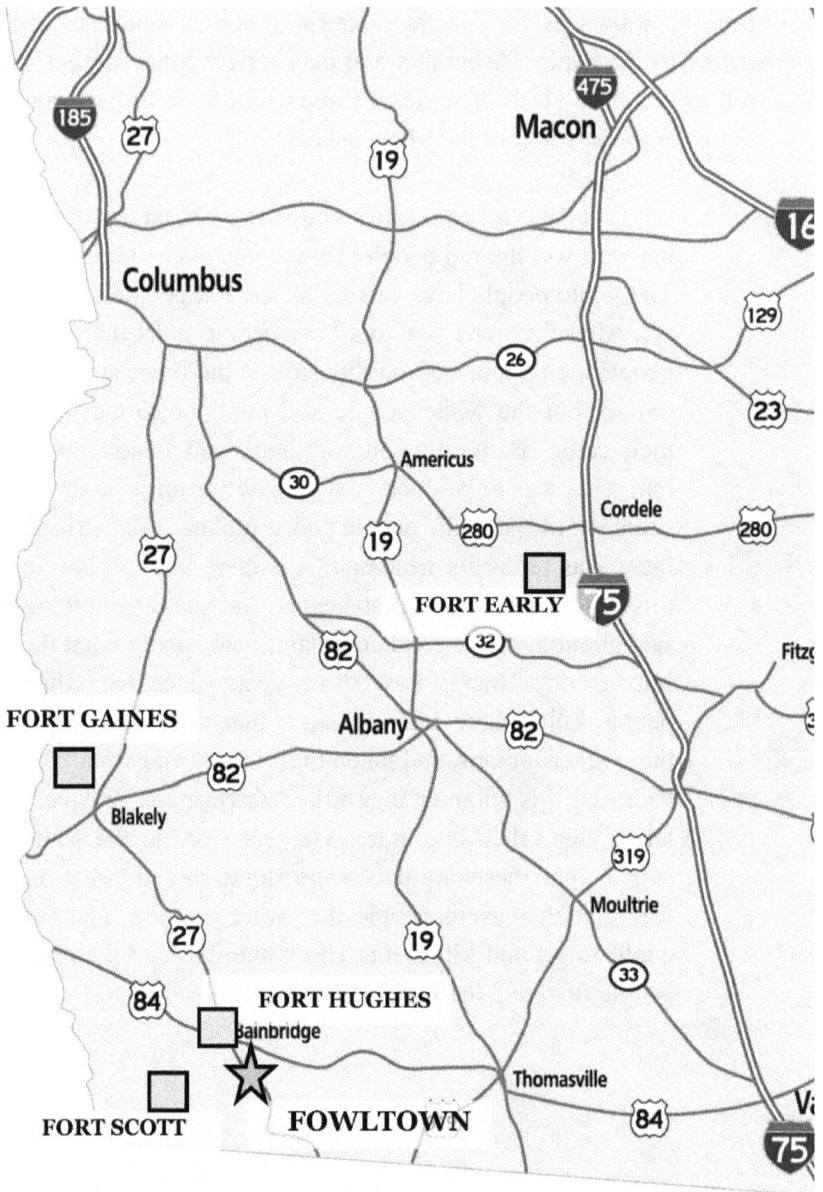

First Seminole War in Georgia

The chief went on to assert that three additional murders by whites had not yet met with retaliation, a statement that Maj. Gen. Gaines took as a threat but one that may not have been intended that way by the old chief.

Cappachimico went on to express the frustration that his people felt with the whites, pointing out that his own complaints always seemed to fall on deaf ears:

> …You have written that there were houses burnt, but we know of no such thing being done; the truth in such cases ought to be told, but this appears otherwise. On that side of the river the white people have killed five Indians, but there is nothing said about that; and all that the Indians have done is brought up. All the mischief the white people have done ought to be told to their headman. When there is any thing done, you write to us, but never write to your headman what the white people do. When the red people send talks, or write, they always send the truth.[132]

The chief did admit that his warriors were responsible for the deaths of Mrs. Garrett and her two children on the St. Marys, but asserted that the killings were justified:

> It appears that all the mischief is laid on this town; but all the mischief that has been done by this town is two horses – one of them is dead, and the other was sent back. The cattle that we are accused of taking were cattle that the white people took from us. Our young men went and brought them back, with the same marks and brands. There were some of our young men out hunting, and they were killed. Others went to take satisfaction, and the kettle of the one that were killed was found in the

---

[132] *Ibid.*

house where the woman and two children were killed; and they supposed it had been her husband who had killed the Indians, and took their satisfaction there. We are accused of killing up Americans, and so on; but since the word was sent to us that peace was made, we stay steady at home and meddle with no person.[133]

Cappachimico concluded by responding to a demand from Gen. Gaines that he surrender up all of the escaped or captured American slaves reported to be living on the Suwannee River. The general did not understand the dynamics then at play among the various Native American groups in North Florida. The Miccosukee chief exerted authority only over his own town and even that was not total. Each town chief was responsible for his town. Neamathla, for example, was chief only over Fowltown while Cappachimico was the senior or principal chief of Miccosukee. The Alachua chief Boleck exerted authority at Suwannee but he did not really control the maroon settlement there. Nero, described as a "negro chief," was the principal man of that community, even though it lay near to Boleck's town. Cappachimico explained to Gaines that he could not help regarding the blacks on the Suwannee:

> …You have sent to us respecting the black people on the Suwanee river. We have nothing to do with them; they were put there by the English, and to them you ought to apply for any thing about them. We do not wish our country desolated by an army passing through it for the concern of other people. The Indians have slaves there, also – a great many of them. When we have an opportunity, we shall apply to the English for them, but we cannot get them now.[134]

---

[133] *Ibid.*
[134] *Ibid.*

The British had given "freedom papers" to any escaped slave willing to fight for King George. The Miccosukee chief was explaining to Gen. Gaines that the Black Seminoles living on the Suwannee River were free and that neither he nor any other Seminole or Miccosukee chief had authority over them. Many of the men had served in the Colonial Marines under Lt. Col. Edward Nicolls and Capt. George Woodbine and had claimed their freedom through their service. Slaves could not be soldiers under British law, only free men could claim such status. Nero, Abraham, Polydore and other former marines had made home for themselves on the Suwannee and were prepared to fight for their human right to freedom.

Maj. Gen. Gaines received Cappachimico's reply at the end of September 1817 and immediately forwarded it on to Maj. Gen. Andrew Jackson in Nashville:

> By this communication it appears that, instead of a compliance with my demand, the chiefs have set up a claim against us for the lives of three Indians, for whom they allege they have not yet taken satisfaction. They charge us with having killed ten of their warriors, and claim a balance of three to be due to them; they admit, by necessary implication, that they have killed seven of our citizens.
>
> They acknowledge the murder of a woman (Mrs. Garrett) and her two children; but the chiefs attempt to justify this act upon the ground that the warriors who committed the outrage had just before lost some friends, had entered our settlements to take satisfaction, found at the house of Garrett a kettle belonging to the Indian that had been killed, and, from that circumstance, supposed the murder had been committed by the husband of the woman; they, therefore, killed her and her two children.[135]

---

[135] Maj. Gen. Edmund P. Gaines to Maj. Gen. Andrew Jackson, October 1, 1817,

Gaines further informed Jackson of Neamathla's warning that U.S. soldiers should not cross to the east side of the Flint River, repeating the chief's statement that he had been "by the Powers above to protect and defend it, and should do so; and it would be seen that talking could not frighten him.." Gaines also relayed intelligence from Maj. Twiggs to the effect that the Fowltown Indians had stolen and killed a herd of 100 cattle from the settlers on the Georgia frontier.[136]

Gaines wrote a second letter to Jackson on the same day – October 1, 1817 – along with an almost identical one to the Secretary of War. In them he explained that he was preparing for war:

> ...I am convinced that nothing but the application of force, will be sufficient to ensure a permanent adjustment of this affair. I shall therefore put the First Brigade in motion for Fort Scott as soon as I can possibly obtain transportation, and I trust that I shall at least by the 20th or 25th reach that place.
>
> As soon as I can obtain transport I shall report to you by Express. My heavy supplies will go by water with suitable guards; the principal part of the force however will go by Land; and in any event we shall finish the new road, near one third of which is already completed...I shall confer with the agent upon the subject of punishing and removing out of our limits these disorderly Indians.[137]

Jackson Papers, Library of Congress.

[136] *Ibid.*

[137] Maj. Gen. Edmund P. Gaines to Maj. Gen. Andrew Jackson, October 1, 1817 (2), Jackson Papers, Library of Congress. See also Gaines to the Secretary of War of the same date.

The general did seem to understand that there was a difference of opinion as to the exact location of the border of the United States as established by the Treaty of Fort Jackson. The whites claimed that they now owned all of Southwest Georgia and what had been Creek territory from the mouth of Cemochechobee Creek to the Florida line. Neamathla and Cappachimico, however, had explained that they believed the border to be the Flint River. Neamathla had asserted this when he told Maj. Twiggs that the land east of the Flint belonged to him. Cappachimico explained further to Gen. Gaines that he and his people had been told to stay "on this side of the river" and had done so. Neither chief explained who identified the Flint River as the line to them but their two independent statements leave little doubt that they were told this by someone.

Gaines suggested to both Jackson and the Secretary of War that the actual line dividing Georgia from Florida should be surveyed from the forks of the Chattahoochee and Flint Rivers to the head of the St. Marys River. Doing so would eliminate any confusion as to the location of the border:

> To put at rest any doubt upon the subject of limits, and to enable us to confine the Indians to their own territory, it is very desirable that the national Boundary should be surveyed and marked from the East bank of the appalachicola river to the Okafonoka Swamp. Should the President be pleased to authorize the work there can be no period more suitable for its execution than the next two months, whilst the troops are in that quarter. This part of the line it will be recollected has never been run. Whether it can or cannot be completed without an agent or Commissioner on the part of Spain, is a question about which I know nothing, but which I presume the President could at once determine.[138]

---

[138] *Ibid.*

The suggestion by Gen. Gaines that the boundary be surveyed became an afterthought as the U.S. military prepared for war against Fowltown and Miccosukee. Maj. Peter Muhlenberg was sent with a detachment to escort two supply ships from Mobile along the Gulf Coast to Apalachicola Bay and then up the Apalachicola River to Fort Scott. Gaines then ordered the main bodies of the 4th and 7th Infantry regiments to prepare to march. They would cross from Fort Crawford to Fort Gaines using the new military road cut by Maj. Twiggs. From the latter post they would continue on to Fort Scott. The general expected them to be in place by the end of October, but it was November 19 before the lead elements arrived at the post on the Flint River. By the time the troops reached Fort Scott, authorization had gone out from the Secretary of War for military action against Fowltown, so long as the army did not cross the border into Spanish Florida:

> …You are authorized to remove the Indians still remaining on the lands ceded by the treaty made by General Jackson with the Creeks; and, in doing so, it may be proper to retain some of them as hostages until reparation may have been made for the depredations which have been committed. McIntosh and the other chiefs of the Creek nation, who were here some time since, expressed then, decidedly, their unwillingness to permit any of the hostile Indians to return to their nation.[139]

The Secretary's authorization did not reach Fort Scott until December 2, 1817. The Seminole Wars had been underway for more than one week by that date.

---

[139] George Graham, acting Secretary of War, to Maj. Gen. Edmund P. Gaines, November 12, 1817, Records of the Adjutant General, Letters Received, National Archives.

11

THE BATTLE OF FOWLTOWN

MAJOR GENERAL EDMUND PENDLETON GAINES reached Fort Scott on November 18, 1817, just ahead of the main bodies of the 4th and 7th U.S. Infantry. He sent a runner to Fowltown with a request that Neamathla come to the post for a face to face conference. The chief refused, telling the courier that he had already said to Maj. David E. Twiggs all that he had to say.

The long-columns of soldiers marched through the gates of the Fort Scott on November 19, 1817. They came down from Fort Gaines by land, opening a road that they called the "Fort Scott Road" but which is known as the "Three Notch Road" today. It provided a direct connection between the two frontier posts that was undoubtedly primitive but sufficiently cleared for army wagons to pass. They arrived exhausted but ready for action and Gaines was quick to oblige. He drafted orders to Maj. Twiggs on the next morning:

> The hostile character & Conduct of the Indians of the Fowl Town, settled within our limits, rendering it absolutely necessary that they should be removed, you will proceed to the town with the detachment assigned you, and remove them. You will arrest and bring the chiefs and warriors to this place, but should they oppose

you, or attempt to escape, you will in that event treat them as enemies. Your men are to be strictly prohibited, in any event, from firing upon, or otherwise injuring, women and children.

You will return to this place with your command as soon as practicable.

Should you receive satisfactory information that any considerable number of the neighboring Indians have joined those of Fowl Town, you will immediately return to this place without making any further attempt to execute first the above written orders.[140]

The written instructions left Neamathla with no real options other than to surrender or fight. If he and his people even tried to run they would be treated as enemies. Gaines did admonish Twiggs not to fire on women and children but in the confusion of a pre-sunrise approach – which is what the two officers planned – such prohibitions would only go so far should the Fowltown warriors resist being surrounded and taken as hostages.

Maj. Twiggs assembled a battalion of 250 men for the march to Fowltown. It is not clear whether he had ever visited the village, but he did at least benefit from the descriptions of couriers who had carried messages there. He knew that the distance from Fort Scott was around 12-miles, three miles less than the standard day's march for the U.S. Army. The crossing of the Flint River would require extra time, however, so the major ordered his men to prepare to move out.

The route of march took the column up the west side of the Flint River via today's 10 Mile Still Road to a point opposite the high ground then known as Burges's Bluff. The name originated from the late 18th and early 19th century trading post operated there by James Burges, a sometimes assistant to Col. Benjamin Hawkins. The trading post stood along the bluff top at present-day Bainbridge, Georgia, and was

---

[140] Maj. Gen. Edmund P. Gaines to Bvt. Maj. David E. Twiggs, November 20, 1817, Adjutant General, Letters Received, National Archives.

associated with the Lower Creek town of Pucknauhitla. Burges had passed away some 10-15 years earlier and his settlement was abandoned, although the ruins of its structures could still be seen. The site had remained in use as a crossing point, but it is unclear whether travelers made it across using a ford or by means of a boat or canoe.[141]

The soldiers would cross the Flint here and then turn back down the east side of the river to arrive outside of Fowltown during the early morning darkness. It was not the most direct route from Fort Scott to the town and Twiggs may have anticipated that this would conceal his movements from Neamathla and his warriors.

The march to Fowltown began on the afternoon of November 20, 1817. As expected, the column marched up the old road or trail to Burges's crossing and appear to have made it across the river with limited difficulty as evening arrived and darkness fell. They turned back down the trail that followed the high ground on the east side of the Flint River and approached Fowltown during the darkest hours of the next morning.

No detailed descriptions of the town are known to exist but it was probably typical of Lower Creek and Miccosukee communities of the time, although perhaps more concentrated because the relocation to the site had taken place only one year earlier. Capt. Hugh Young, an army topographer who passed with Jackson's army in 1818, wrote a brief description of Fowltown that relied on the accounts of officers who had been there:

> Fowl Town. The last settlement of these Indians was twelve miles east of Fort Scott, in a tolerable body of land. They had between thirty and forty warriors and their chief Innematla was a man of talents and courage. In manners, trade and agriculture they were similar to the Mikasukees. Formerly the Fowl Towns were neatly

---

[141] Mark F. Boyd, "Historic Sites in and around the Jim Woodruff Reservoir," *River Basin Surveys Papers*, No. 13, Smithsonian, 1958:

but after their settlement near Fort Scott they had few cattle and depended on their crops and hunting for subsistene. This tribe had the arts of spinning and weaving which they learned before their expulsion from the upper Creeks. In character, they were perfidious, cowardly and mischievous.[142]

Young's account is consistent with the view of Fowltown's inhabitants that was held by most officers and soldiers of the time. His claim that they were "perfidious, cowardly and mischievous" was based almost entirely on Neamathla's unwillingness to surrender his people's land without a fight.

The weather was cold and frosty as the soldiers moved through the night on their way to Fowltown. Ice formed in the streets of Charleston, South Carolina, that night as the first cold front of the season swept down through the Southeast. Temperatures had been unseasonably warm all month but began to plunge on the 19th as the 4th and 7th Regiments reached Fort Scott. The night of the 20th was seasonably cold, especially as the soldiers moved down into the broad basin of Fowltown Swamp and Four Mile Creek. The creek flows out of the swamp just over one mile east of the Flint River and then runs in a slightly northwest directly to its confluence with the Flint. The route of the march from Burges's down to the swamp likely followed a trail shown on the 1819 District Plats of Survey on file at the Georgia Archives. This pathway or "road" ran parallel to the Flint River about half way between the east bank and today's Faceville Road (GA 97).[143]

Neamathla was not expecting an attack by U.S. troops and no warriors had been placed to guard his town from surprise. This allowed

---

[142] Capt. Hugh Young, "A Topographical Memoir of East and West Florida, with Itineraries," 1819, Records of Reports, July 3, 1812 – October 4, 1823, pp. 292-336, Records of the Chief of Engineers, National Archives.

[143] *Charleston City* Gazette, November 20, 1817; District Plat of Survey, Early County, District 20, October 5, 1825 (copied from 1819 plat), Survey Records, Surveyor General, RG 3-3-24, Georgia Archives.

Twiggs to approach the town undetected and begin to form his companies for an enveloping movement:

> …Having marched all the night of the 20th I reached the town before day light on the morning of the 21st & posted the troops in order of Battle intending silently to surround it & without blood shed bring to you the chief & warriors, but they fled from the companies of Majr. Montgomery & Cpt. Birch on my right & fired upon my left under Capts. Allison & Bee when they were fired on in return. Discovering my superiority of force they fled to a neighboring swamp.[144]

The exchange of fire between Neamathla's warriors and the soldiers of Bee's and Allison's companies on Twiggs's right flank was the first of the Seminole Wars. Fighting would continue with occasional interruption for the next 41 years.

Fowltown had been taken by complete surprise and the firing on both sides was wild. No soldiers were wounded and Twiggs reported that the Creeks had lost "but few as they received but one round & fled." He did not provide estimates of Native American losses in his brief written report of the affair, but apparently told Gen. Gaines that the fire of Neamathla's men "was briskly returned by the detachment, and the Indians put to flight with the loss of four warriors slain – and, as there is reason to believe, many more wounded."[145]

Gaines wrote to Maj. Gen. Andrew Jackson on the day of the attack, informing him of the skirmish and reporting that the village's casualties included at least one woman:

---

[144] Bvt. Maj. David E. Twiggs to Maj. Gen. Edmund P. Gaines, November 21, 1817, Records of the Adjutant General's Office, Letters Received, National Archives.

[145] *Ibid.*; Maj. Gen. Edmund P. Gaines to Gov. Peter Early, November 21, 1817, published in the *New York Commercial Advertiser*, December 15, 1817.

It is with deep regret I have to add that a woman was accidentally shot with some warriors in the act of forcing their way through our line formed for the purpose of arresting their flight. The unfortunate woman had a blanket fastened round her (as many of the warriors had) which amidst the smoke in which they were enveloped, rendered it impossible, as I am assured by the officers present, to distinguish her from the warriors.[146]

The Native American account of the attack was included in a letter from Cappachimico and Boleck to Gov. Charles Cameron in the Bahamas. The document appears to have been written for them by Alexander Arbuthnot and is somewhat garbled. The part that appears to refer to the pre-dawn attack of November 21 begins with a mention of the letter sent to Cappachimico by Gen. Gaines:

...This letter only appears to have been a prelude to plans determined on by the said General and General Jackson, to bring on troops and settlers, to drive us from our lands; and take possession of them; for, in the end of [November], a party of Americans surrounded Fowl Town during the night, and in the morning began setting fire to it; making the unfortunate inhabitants fly to the swamps, and who in their flight had three persons killed by the fire of the Americans.[147]

The troops remained in Fowltown only until daybreak. Maj. Twiggs reported that they did not destroy the town but left it intact. He did report to Gen. Gaines that a significant quantity of corn was seen in the corncribs of the village and that he and his officers had inspected

---

[146] Maj. Gen. Edmund P. Gaines to Maj. Gen. Andrew Jackson, November 21, 1817, Jackson Papers, Library of Congress.

[147] Cappiahimico and Bowlegs to Gov. Cameron, n.d., included in *The Trials of A. Arbuthnot and R.C. Ambrister*, London, 1819: 19-21.

Neamathla's home. There, according to the general, they found "a British uniform coat (Scarlet) with a pair of gold Epaulettes, and a certificate signed by a british Captain of Marines." The certificate noted that Neamathla had always been a "true and faithful friend to the British" and was signed by Capt. Robert White of the Royal Marines.[148]

Twiggs returned to Fort Scott with his battalion on the same day as the skirmish, taking with him little besides a few horses and a few head of cattle. He reported to Gen. Gaines that his men and officers all performed well in what was for many their baptism of fire.[149]

The skirmish was not really a battle and Neamathla showed no immediate signs of retaliating. After speaking with Maj. Twiggs and his officers on the night of the 21st and morning of the 22nd, Gaines decided to send a second, larger force back to the village. The mission was entrusted to Lt. Col. Matthew Arbuckle of the 7th Infantry. He left Fort Scott that afternoon, deciding to approach the town from a different direction than had Twiggs. The general reported that the purpose of the raid was "to ascertain the strength of the hostile Indians in the vicinity of Fowltown, and to reconnoiter the adjacent country."[150]

Lt. Col. Arbuckle started his men crossing the Flint River at Fort Scott on the afternoon of November 22, 1817. They would march up the east side of the river and approach Fowltown from the south. This may have been due to advice from Maj. Twiggs, who saw that the main town was on the south side of Four Mile Creek. The warriors would be much more alert this time and the route chosen by Arbuckle would spare his men the danger of ambush that a crossing through the swamp would create. The route of march undoubtedly followed the "Federal Trail" shown on the 1819 plats. From Fort Scott it led up out of the swamps to firmer ground but generally stayed within shouting distance of the Flint River all the way to Burges's Bluff north of Fowltown.[151]

---

[148] Gaines to Jackson, November 21, 1817.

[149] *Ibid.*

[150] Maj. Gen. Edmund P. Gaines to the Secretary of War, November 26, 1817, *American State Papers – Indian Affairs*, Part II: 160.

The column included 300 soldiers from the 4th and 7th Infantry regiments. The reports do not make mention of an artillery presence, but artillerymen were among the troops forming Arbuckle's command. Lt. Milo Johnson of Capt. Sanders Donoho's company, 4th Artillery, took part in the battle and the soldiers may have carried at least one of his unit's field pieces with them.[152]

Arbuckle's command halted at some point during the night to rest for a few hours. This guaranteed that the men would be fresh for the battle while also delaying their arrival at Fowltown until well after sunrise. This was probably an intentional way of avoiding the confusion of fighting in the darkness should Neamathla once again resist the presence of the soldiers. It was late morning by the time the troops came within site of the village:

> ...The town which is about eighteen miles distant from this place and four from the Bluff we entered on the 23 Instant about 10 O'clock in the morning without opposition. On our approach several signal guns were fired by the Indians who no doubt discovered one of our flanking parties but at the time that all the troops had reached the town no Indians were seen and a few yells only were heard from a swamp which skirts its north east side. I took a position near the town so as to secure the troops from any fire which might issue from the swamp, and after posting such sentinels as would prevent us

---

[151] District Plats of Survey, Early County, Districts 15, 20 & 21, 1825 (copied from 1819 plat), Survey Records, Surveyor General, RG 3-3-24, Georgia Archives.

[152] Lt. Milo Johnson to Maj. Gen. Edmund P. Gaines, November 30, 1817, Records of the Office of the Adjutant General, Letters Received, National Archives; Artifacts on display at the Decatur County Historical Society Museum in Bainbridge, Georgia, include a small cannonball found at a site near Four Mile Creek.

from being surprised I ordered the men to refresh themselves while the waggons were loading with corn.[153]

Arbuckle was by nature a much more cautious officer than Maj. Twiggs. The fact that he approached Fowltown with flanking parties out is clear evidence that he was taking all proper steps to avoid being surprised. Such steps had likely been reinforced prior to his departure from Fort Scott by Gen. Gaines, who routinely cautioned officers under his command to be vigilant and careful.

The soldiers knew that Neamathla and his warriors were in the swamp and watching them but the intensity of the attack still took them by surprise when it hit:

> ...[The loading of the wagons] was done and the troops were about to march when the Indians, fifty or sixty in number (as I judge) were perceived advancing by the sentinels posted in the swamp and fired on: The fire was instantly returned by the Indians who giving the War Hoop advanced rapidly towards our lines. Parties were immediately detached to take possession of the houses between our position and the swamp which movement checked the progress of the Indians and compelled them to fall back. A spirited fire was then kept up for twenty or twenty five minutes when the Indians retreated into the Swamp. During the affair the Indians frequently appeared in the open ground and from the number which were seen to fall, there can be no doubt but six or eight were killed and many severely wounded yet as the swamp was large and uncommonly thick I deemed it not prudent to pursue them into it or search for those who fell on its edges.[154]

---

[153] Lt. Col. Matthew Arbuckle to Maj. Gen. Edmund P. Gaines, November 30, 1817, Jackson Papers, Library of Congress.
[154] *Ibid.*

Arbuckle was surprised that Neamathla would attack a much larger force over open ground. The intensity of the attack also took him off guard. The officer did not realize, however, that the corn stocks in the village were vital to the survival of men, women and children through the coming winter. The town had relocated three times in four years. Its once extensive herds of cattle were gone and the corncribs likely meant the difference between life and death for many in the community. The warriors were fighting to save their homes and families and did so against odds of roughly 6 to 1:

> ...A spirited fire was then kept up for twenty or twenty five minutes when the Indians retreated into the Swamp. During the affair the Indians frequently appeared in the open ground and from the number which were seen to fall, there can be no doubt but six or eight were killed and many severely wounded yet as the swamp was large and uncommonly thick I deemed it not prudent to pursue them into it or search for those who fell on its edges. The skill and valor displayed by the officers and men engaged in the little affair affords a pleasing prospect should their services be required on another important occasion. The Indians must have been deceived as to our numbers otherwise they should not have had the temerity to attack us.[155]

Whether all of the officers and soldiers fought as valiantly as Arbuckle indicated is subject to some debate. Rumors swirled after the battle that Lt. Milo Johnson of the 4th Artillery had not performed well in action. Johnson had graduated from the U.S. Military Academy at West Point in the Class of 1815. Notable officers to come from that class included Gen. Samuel Cooper, who became the highest-ranking Confederate officer, and Col. William Chase, who supervised

---

[155] *Ibid.*

construction of Fort Pickens at Pensacola, Florida. Johnson requested a chance to defend himself against the allegations being made against him:

> Having understood that a report is calculating through the camp, that I behaved unlike a soldier in being separated from my compy. and while separated in the affair at Fowl Town, on the 23d of Nov. 1817. I am compelled in justice to myself to demand a court of enquiry, to investigate the truth of sd. report.[156]

No further explanation of his actions during the battle has been found and there is no evidence in the available military records that a court martial was ever convened in his case. Subsequent events quickly overshadowed the Battle of Fowltown and Johnson's conduct – whatever it might have been – was forgotten.

Lt. Johnson's mention of his company appears to indicate that Capt. Donoho's artillery company was present at the Battle of Fowltown, even though it is not specifically mentioned in the official reports. The unit did have several field guns, the largest of which was a 6-pounder. The deployment of at least one of these guns during the fighting would explain the discovery of a solid shot near Four Mile Creek. The cannonball is too small to date from the Civil War and there was no other recorded action in the area from which it could date.

The Native American account of the battle was simple. Boleck and Cappachimico wrote – likely through Alexander Arbuthnot – in a letter to Gov. Charles Cameron in the Bahamas that Fowltown had been attacked by American soldiers. "Our Indians, rallying, drove the Americans from the town," they reported, "but in their exertions had two more people killed."[157]

---

[156] Lt. Milo Johnson to Maj. Gen. Edmund P. Gaines, November 30, 1817, Records of the Office of the Adjutant General, Letters Received.

[157] Cappachimico and Bowlegs to Gov. Charles Cameron, n.d., *The Trials of A. Arbuthnot and R.C. Ambrister*, London, 1819: 19-20.

The chiefs did not report the number of warriors who were wounded in the fighting, but U.S. soldiers reported seeing several fall along the edges of the swamp. Lt. Col. Arbuckle listed his own losses as 1 killed and 2 wounded. The soldier who lost his life at Fowltown was Pvt. Aaron Hughes, a regimental musician. He had joined the army at the age of 15 and served through the War of 1812 without injury. He was reportedly shot while trying to rally the troops by standing on an Indian cabin and playing his fife.[158]

The firefight lasted 15-20 minutes and ended when Neamathla and his men withdrew deeper into the swamp. Arbuckle described what happened next as a "march" but officers in his command said it was a "retreat." The soldiers definitely moved quickly from the town and marched up the trail to Burges's Bluff (Bainbridge):

> The detachment consisted of 300 men, under the command of Colonel Arbucle. They were attacked about twelve miles from Fort Scott, by a party of Fowltown and Osouche Indians, supposed to be about one hundred, and had one man killed and two wounded, one dangerously. The Indian loss was supposed to be eight or ten. They captured some cattle during the flight, which were retaken in the towns, lying about eight miles from Fort Scot. – The detachment then retreated four miles and threw up breast works.[159]

Another officer described the battle in similar terms when he wrote to his father from Fort Scott on December 2, 1817:

> I marched from Fort Hawkins on the 15th Nov. and arrived here on the 19th, at night. On the 23d, Col. Arbuckle crossed Flint river with 300 men, for the

---

[158] Mark F. Boyd, "Historic Sites in and around the Jim Woodruff Reservoir."
[159] Officer to the Editors, *Georgia Journal*, December 2,1817.

purpose of destroying an Indian town, about 20 miles off. We arrived in the town about 12 o'clock, next day – at 3, the Indians attacked us, and after an action of about 15 minutes, they retreated into a large swamp which nearly surrounded their town. – The loss cannot be ascertained – Ours, 1 killed, 1 severely and 3 slightly wounded.[160]

The brief account provided by Cappachimico and Boleck ("Bowlegs") appears to indicate that Neamathla attacked the retreating soldiers somewhere between Fowltown and Burges's Bluff and recovered some of the stolen cattle. None of the U.S. accounts are known to mention such an encounter but the beef was vital to the survival of the Tutalosis and a raid or quick strike to recover some of it makes sense.

The battle over, the troops marched north on the "Federal trail" to Burges's Bluff where they buried Aaron Hughes and began to build a new fort. It was 90-feet square with blockhouses on two diagonal corners. Lt. Col. Arbuckle named it Fort Hughes after the unfortunate musician. Detachments went out to reconnoiter and round up more supplies as the work of building the outpost went forward:

> The scite of the Fort is on a Bluff sixty or seventy feet above the River and distant about one hindred yards from its edge, the space between the fort and the River and for a considerable distance above and below is very open from this position both on and off the River. There is a considerable portion of good land. The surface of the country is very pleasant and from every appearance must be healthy. This I consider a very advantageous position for a post, it being eight or ten miles nearer to Fort Gaines than this place is and more than that distance

---

[160] Officer to his Father, December 2, 1817, *New York Daily Advertiser*, December 27, 1817.

nearer to that portion of the Creeks who have commenced the war. During the time I was detained at the Bluff I had small parties reconnoitering every day and from the number of fresh trails reported to lead in a direction for Fort Gaines there can be no doubt that an understanding exists between the hostile Indians and those residing on the Chattahoochie and that a considerable number of the latter will join the hostile party. On our tour we took from the hostile Indians for horses, fifteen head of cattle, and about Eighty bushels of corn.[161]

It took Arbuckle's command 3-4 days to complete the small fort. The column then crossed the Flint River at Burges's and returned to Fort Scott. Capt. John N. McIntosh was left in command at Fort Hughes with a detachment of 40 men, a number believed sufficient for the defense of the post.[162]

It is fairly remarkable that Lt. Col. Arbuckle and other officers claimed that the Creek warriors of Fowltown "commenced the war." Neamathla and his followers had been peacefully sleeping in their homes when U.S. troops arrived and tried to surround their village. It is true that they opened fire first, but it was only as soldiers approached in the darkness of night and began to encircle them. Gov. Mitchell, the new Indian Agent, saw things differently from the officers at Fort Scott. He reported that three towns had agreed to a talk delivered at Fort Hawkins in July, even though they had been unable to attend:

> Of the three towns referred to, Fowl Town was one; but before I had an opportunity of sending for those Chiefs, or of taking any measures to meet their

---

[161] Lt. Col. Matthew Arbuckle to Maj. Gen. Edmund P. Gaines, November 30, 1814.
[162] *Ibid.*

proposition, Gen. Gaines arrived with a detachment of troops from the west – sent for the Chief of Fowl Town, and for his contumacy in not immediately appearing before him, the town was attacked and destroyed by the troops of the United States, by order of Gen. Gaines. The fact was, I conceive, the immediate cause of the war. [163]

Mitchell seems to have been confused about the identity of the three towns that agreed to the terms of his talk at Fort Hawkins. They were Ekanachatte, Tocktoethla and Ocheese Talofa. Fowltown was not among them. Otherwise his statement was likely correct. The attack on Fowltown most definitely was the spark that ignited the First Seminole War.

---

[163] Gov. David B. Mitchell, testimony regarding the Seminole War, quoted in "Philo Pacificus," *Friend of Peace*, Volume II, Cambridge, 1821: 16.

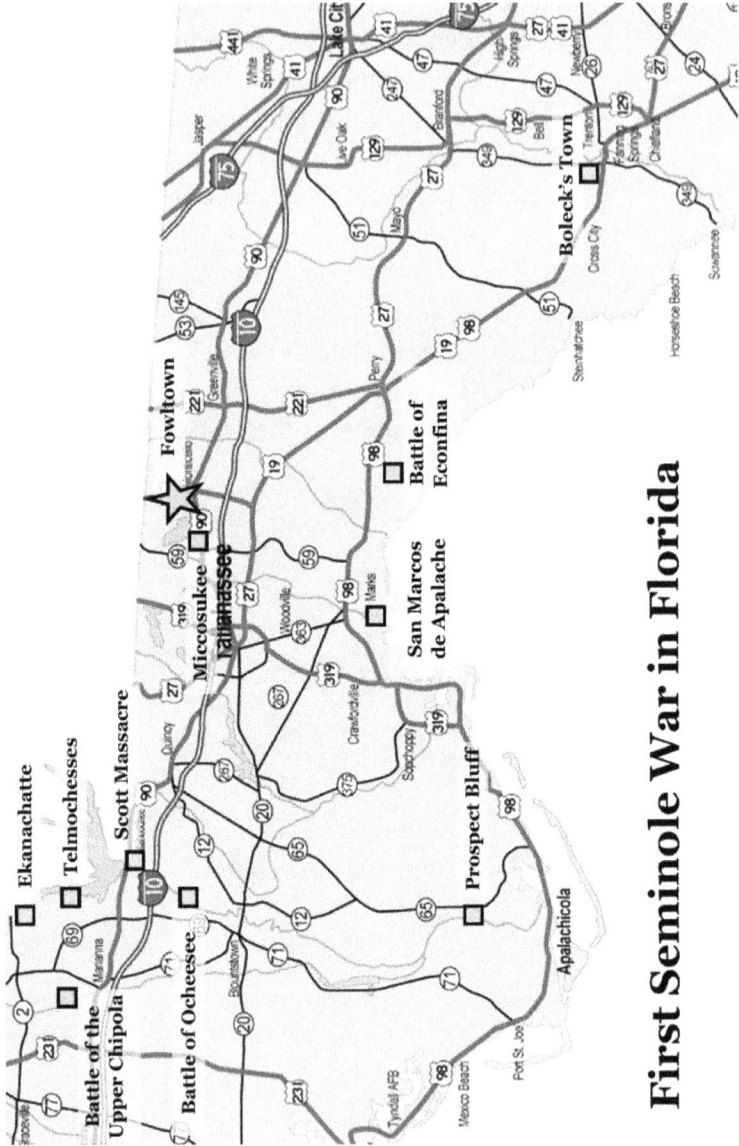

First Seminole War in Florida

12

THE END OF FOWLTOWN

THE U.S. ARMY RAIDS ON FOWLTOWN were failures. The objectives, as outlined by Maj. Gen. Edmund P. Gaines, were to forcibly remove the inhabitants of the town from lands ceded to the United States by the Treaty of Fort Jackson and to take Neamathla, the other chiefs and the warriors prisoner and bring them to Fort Scott. Neither Maj. David E. Twiggs nor Lt. Col. Matthew Arbuckle achieved these aims. They did succeed, however, in stirring up a hornet's nest of anger among most of the Lower Creek, Seminole, Red Stick Creek, Miccosukee and Black Seminole towns in the borderlands of Spanish Florida. Those groups would soon strike back with a fury that the army neither expected nor was prepared to handle.

News of the first attack at Fowltown was followed quickly by word of the second raid and the battle that it ignited. Even as Cappachimico and Boleck met with Alexander Arbuthnot to draft a request for help to Gov. Charles Cameron in the Bahamas, warriors from the region marched to reinforce Neamathla. The Red Sticks were prominent in this movement, as were the Black Seminoles who lived near Boleck's town on the Suwannee. Robert C. Armbrister, a former lieutenant in the British Colonial Marines, ordered a white Bahamian named Peter Cook to lead warriors from the Suwannee River to the Flint. Cook had previously been Arbuthnot's assistant, but had joined forces with Armbrister when the latter arrived in the region as part of former Capt. George Woodbine's mysterious activities in Florida during the years following the War of 1812.[164]

Command of this assembling army was assigned to the Prophet Josiah Francis who had arrived back in Florida after his unsuccessful journey to Great Britain to lobby for a permanent alliance between the British and the Florida Indians. The warriors were not well-supplied with ammunition although most carried British muskets and other equipment provided to them by Lt. Col. Edward Nicolls during the War of 1812. Peter McQueen, Homathlemico and other Red Stick chiefs joined Francis in martialing the warriors who had fought under them since the Creek War of 1813-1814. The strategy that soon developed was three-pronged. Homathlemico would lead several hundred Red Stick warriors and Black Seminoles to the forks of the Chattahoochee and Flint Rivers, where he would attempt to block any supply vessels already on their way upstream to Fort Scott. Francis would go to Spanish Bluffs in today's Calhoun County, Florida, where he would capture Edmund Doyle and William Hambly. Doyle had evacuated the John Forbes & Company trading post at Prospect Bluff due to rising tensions and gone to Hambly's plantation at Spanish Bluffs. Once he captured the two traders, Francis would position the main body of his army at Ocheesee Bluff where he could block additional supply ships trying to make their way up to Fort Scott and Fort Gaines. Finally, Peter Cook would lead the force under his command to Fort Hughes, the new outpost thrown up by Lt. Col. Arbuckle at Burges's Bluff following the Battle of Fowltown, and attempt to take the stockade. Other warriors would hover around Fort Scott to keep the soldiers there pinned down while smaller parties would strike along the roads leading to Forts Scott and Gaines.

---

[164] Peter Cook to Elizabeth Carney, January 19, 1818, *American State Papers – Foreign Relations*, Volume IV: 605. For more information on the activities of Armbrister and Arbuthnot, please see *The Trials of A. Arbuthnot and R.C. Ambrister*, London, 1819. Note: Armbrister's name was spelled "Ambrister" in many early documents and is often repeated that way today. Recent scholarship, however, suggests that Armbrister is the correct spelling.

Homathlemico was the first to arrive at the front. He concentrated his force at the old earthworks of Nicolls' Outpost – called "Fort Apalachicola" by U.S. officers at Fort Scott – and was soon joined there by many of the Fowltown warriors under Chenubby (Chinnabee?), the war chief of the village. Neamathla was likely engaged in trying to get the woman, children and other noncombatants of his village to safety. Homathlemico knew from local warriors that a military boat was making its way upstream after leaving two large supply ships that were coming up the Apalachicola at a slower pace.

The warriors likely did not know it, but the vessel they prepared to intercept was commanded by 1st Lt. Richard W. Scott of Twiggs' Company, 7th U.S. Infantry. He had been sent down from Fort Scott after arriving there with one boat-load of supplies from Mobile to locate and assist the delayed flotilla under Maj. Peter Muhlenberg. Instead of keeping all of Scott's able-bodied men, however, Muhlenberg exchanged half of his detachment for around the same number of sick and unarmed men from his own command and ordered the lieutenant to carry them up to Fort Scott. Seven women – the wives of soldiers – and four children were also placed on board Scott's boat. This was counter to orders from Gen. Gaines that Muhlenberg should "keep your vessels close together," but the major had no way of knowing that actual hostilities had erupted.[165]

Scott reached Spanish Bluffs on November 28, 1817. He was met there by William Hambly, who warned that serious danger was assembling just ahead:

> ...Mr. Hambly informs me that Indians are assembling at the junction of the river, where they intend to make a stand against those vessels coming up the river. Should this be the case, I am not able to make a stand against

---

[165] Maj. Gen. Edmund P. Gaines to Maj. Gen. Andrew Jackson, December 2, 1817, Jackson Papers, Library of Congress; Maj. Gen. Edmund P. Gaines to Maj. Peter Muhlenberg, November 18, 1817, *American State Papers – Foreign Affairs*, Volume IV: 599.

them. My command does not exceed forty men, and one-half sick and without arms. I leave this immediately.[166]

Why Scott would continue forward knowing that he might encounter an enemy force too large to repel is one of the great mysteries of the First Seminole War. Hambly clearly tried to stop him and even insisted that Scott send a courier overland to Fort Scott with an explanation of the situation that he faced. The courier, however, had to evade the men who were flocking to the Apalachicola River and it took him two days instead of the normal one to reach the fort and deliver the lieutenant's message to Gen. Gaines. By that time, it was too late.

The U.S. Army boat commanded by Lt. Richard W. Scott rounded a sharp bend just one-mile below the confluence of the Chattahoochee and Flint Rivers on the morning of November 30, 1817. The river was running high and the current forced the vessel close to the east bank. A massive volley of gunfire suddenly erupted from the shore. The magnitude of the disaster that followed shocked even the seasoned Gen. Gaines:

> ...It is now my painful duty to report an affair of a more serious and decisive nature than has heretofore occurred, and which leaves no doubt of the necessity of an immediate application of force and active measures on our part. A large party of Seminole Indians, on the 30th ultimo, formed an ambuscade, upon the Appalachicola river, a mile below the junction of the Flint and Chatahouchee, attacked one of our boats, ascending the river near the shore, and killed, wounded, and took, the greater part of the detachment, consisting of forty men, commanded by Lieut. R.W. Scott of the 7th infantry. There were also on board, killed or taken, seven women,

---

[166] Lt. Richard W. Scott to Maj. Gen. Edmund P. Gaines, November 28, 1817, *American State Papers – Foreign Affairs*, Volume IV: 599.

the wives of soldiers. Six men of the detachment only escaped, four of whom were wounded. They report that the strength of the current, at the point of attack, had obliged the lieutenant to keep his boat near the shore; that the Indians had formed along the bank of the river, and were not discovered until their fire commenced; in the first volley of which Lieutenant Scott and his most valuable men fell.[167]

Lt. Scott, 33 of his men, 6 women and 4 children were killed in the attack. Four U.S. soldiers were wounded but survived (some accounts say five were wounded). Two other soldiers escaped by swimming underwater. The attackers also captured a young woman named Elizabeth Stewart, who was knocked unconscious in the battle but saved from death by a warrior who had once been treated kindly by a white woman in St. Marys. He had fallen ill with a fever and she nursed him to health. He repaid her by saving Elizabeth's life.[168]

Fowltown warriors had played a key role in the Scott Massacre, retaliating for the attacks on their town and the deaths of four men and one woman in those raids. Peter Cook, who soon arrived on the Flint with his men from the Suwannee, wrote the only known account of the battle from the Native American perspective. He spoke with warriors who had taken part in the action:

> …There was a boat that was taken by the Indians, that had in it thirty men, seven women, and four small children; there were six of the men got clear, and one woman saved, and all the rest of them got killed; the

---

[167] Maj. Gen. Edmund P. Gaines to George Graham, Secretary of War, December 2, 1817, *American State Papers – Military Affairs*, Volume 1: 687-688.
[168] For a complete account of this battle, please see Dale Cox, *The Scott Massacre of 1817*, Bascom, Florida 2013.

children were taken by the heels, and their brains dashed
out against the boat.[169]

Additional retaliation came on December 10, 1817, when forces
under the Prophet Francis took William Hambly's plantation at Spanish
Bluffs. Hambly and Doyle were taken prisoner while William Perryman
was killed. Perryman was the chief who had requested a council at Fort
Scott in August at which he planned to flog Neamathla for his opposition
to the United States. He had gone down to Hambly's with his warriors in
order to protect the two traders but lost his life in a losing battle to do so.
The Red Sticks forces Perryman's surviving warriors to join their party.[170]

Peter Cook's party arrived on the front after a seven day march. He
gave his men a change to rest and prepare for action while he
coordinated with the other chiefs in the vicinity. A decision was made to
carry out a two-pronged attack against U.S. forces. One prong, under
Cook, would attack Fort Hughes on December 15, 1817. The other
prong, led by the Prophet Francis, would strike Muhlenburg's supply
ships on the same day. The decision to attack Fort Hughes was likely
pushed by the chiefs of Fowltown. As Neamathla had repeatedly
explained to officers at Fort Scott, he believed that the lands east of the
Flint River was his and any intrusions there would be opposed by force.
Fowltown warriors probably joined in that attack, which Cook described:

> …We are threatened every day by the d----d Americans;
> not threatened only, but they have made an attempt,
> which we have stopped. On 1st December I marched
> with thirty men to go against them. After seven days'
> march we arrived at the fort; and after our men got
> rested, I went against it. We had an engagement for four

---

[169] Peter Cook to Elizabeth Carney, January 19, 1818, *American State Papers –
Foreign Affairs*, Volume IV: 605.
[170] Lt. Col. Matthew Arbuckle to Maj. Gen. Edmund P. Gaines, December 20,
1817, *American State Papers – Military Affairs*, Volume I: 689-690.

> hours, and seeing that we could do no good with them, we retreated and came off. The balls flew like hailstones; there was a ball that had like to have done my job; it just cleared by breast. For six days and six nights we had to encamp in the wild woods, and it was constantly raining night and day; and as for the cold, I suffered very much by it; in the morning the water would be frozen about an inch thick.[171]

Fort Hughes was so compact that Capt. John N. McIntosh's small garrison of 40 men was able to defend it against Cook's attack. With the main assault repelled, the attackers continued to fire on the fort for three or four days before melting away into the forest. They were not able to take the outpost, but achieved their goals nonetheless. Lt. Col. Arbuckle, now in command at Fort Scott, became convinced that he could not supply or support Fort Hughes so he ordered it abandoned. Capt. Donoho was sent with 2 sergeants, 2 corporals and 60 privates to extract McIntosh's garrison and bring the men back to Fort Scott. The history of Fort Hughes as a U.S. Army installation had lasted only three weeks.[172]

The second prong of the coordinated attack hit at Ocheesee Bluff when Maj. Muhlenberg's heavy supply vessels entered an S-shaped curve of the Apalachicola River. Hundreds of warriors led by the Prophet Francis opened fire from both sides of the river:

> On Monday morning the transports were attacked by Indians from both sides of the river with a heavy fire of small arms. We returned their fire, the firing has continued ever since. We have lost two men killed and thirteen wounded, most of them severely. Whether we

---

[171] Peter Cook to Elizabeth Carney, January 19, 1818.

[172] Register of Details for Command from Fort Scott, from the 18th of December, 1817, until the 19th of March, 1818, whilst under the command of Lt. Col. Arbuckle, Office of the Adjutant General, Letters Received, National Archives.

have injured them any I am not able to say. We are now compelled to remain here, as it is impossible for us to carry out a warp, as a man cannot shew himself above the bulwarks without being fired on. I can assure you that our present situation is not the most Pleasant not knowing how soon or whether we are to receive succor from above, the wounded are but in a bad situation owing to the vessels being much crowded, and it is impossible to make them any ways comfortable on board.[173]

Francis was not able to take the supply ships – one of which was the *General Pike* which had taken part in the attack on the "Negro Fort at Prospect Bluff in 1816 – but kept them pinned down in the center of the river for nearly two weeks.

Supplies grew short at Fort Scott by the end of the year and Lt. Col. Arbuckle resolved to make one more raid on Fowltown. Corn was desperately needed at the fort. The lieutenant colonel also needed intelligence on what Neamathla and his warriors were doing. With these objectives in mind he left Fort Scott on January 4, 1818, and marched up the road to Burges's Bluff and the abandoned Fort Hughes:

> On the 4th inst. I crossed the Flint River about fourteen miles above this post and proceeded to Fowl Town, which had been deserted. I burnt it, and on the next day arrived at Attapulgis a small town about fourteen miles south east of this post, it had also been abandoned, and the cattle and stock of every kind removed, as had been the case at Foul Town. I am informed they have gone to or beyond the Oaklocny River, there to place their women and property in greater

---

[173] Maj. Peter Muhlenberg to Lt. Col. Matthew Arbuckle, December 16, 1817, Office of the Adjutant General, Letters Received, National Archives.

security, and better prepare themselves for war. They continue to have considerable intercourse with the Indians on the Chatahooche, many of whom were with them and assisted in the destruction of Lieut. Scott and his party, and in the attack on our vessels ascending the river under the command of Brevt. Major Muhlenberg.[174]

Fowltown's history was nearly over. Neamathla led his people from Four Mile Creek on an exodus to Spanish Florida where they settled first on the east side of Lake Miccosukee in what is now Jefferson County. They were attacked there by Gen. Gaines during Jackson's 1818 invasion of Florida. The general led his men across the lake at a point where it was 700 yards wide and 2-3 feet deep. The column then marched two miles to a small village on the margin of the pond, but it was found to be abandoned. From there, they turned east to the new site of Fowltown:

> …[T]hence eastward to Fowl town, where the public square was barbarously decorated with several human scalps which appeared to have been taken from both sexes of our citizens, in the course of the last six months…The town had been abandoned by the enemy and stript of every species of moveable property excepting a few bushels of corn and some few poultry, previous to my arrival. Having witnessed with you, and the Aarmy, at the public square of the principal town on this side [i.e. Miccosukee itself], the proceeding evening, the savage exhibition of the scalps of a number of the citizens of our country not only of men, but of women and infants, I could not hesitate to destroy the dens of those barbarians. Their towns were accordingly burned.[175]

---

[174] Lt. Col. Matthew Arbuckle to Maj. Gen. Andrew Jackson, January 12, 1818, Jackson Papers, Library of Congress.
[175] Maj. Gen. Edmund P. Gaines to Maj. Gen. Andrew Jackson, April 3, 1818, Jackson Papers, Library of Congress.

The only fighting took place as the troops were approaching Fowltown. William McIntosh, now bearing the title of brigadier general in the Creek Brigade, was moving with 300 of his men ahead of the regular troops and militia when he encountered a small group of warriors. They quickly routed this party, killing one Black Seminole warrior and capturing a few others. Gaines learned from the prisoners that Fowltown had been abandoned several hours before his arrival. McIntosh was sent on with 300 of his warriors to attack any other villages or camps found in the area with orders to return to Jackson's main encampment as soon as possible.[176]

The destruction of the town four miles east of Lake Miccosukee marked the end of Fowltown. Neamathla soon resurfaced on the modern site of Tallahassee but his new town there was called Cohowofooche. So far as is known, the name Tutalosi Talofa or Fowltown was never again given to a Muscogee (Creek) or Seminole village.

Neamathla remained prominent in frontier affairs for two decades to come. He begrudgingly allowed a new capitol building to be built near his town by the whites after Florida became a U.S. Territory and his relations with Gov. William P. Duval were chronicled by the author Washington Irving. The aging chief spoke on behalf of many of the Miccosukees and Seminoles in 1823 when he delivered a poignant speech on the treaty grounds at Moultrie Creek:

> We are poor and needy; we do not come here to murmur or complain; we want advice and assistance; we rely upon your justice and humanity; we hope that you will not send us south, to a country where neither the hickorynut, the acorn, nor the persimmon grows; we depend much upon these productions of the forest for food: in the south they are not to be found. For me, I am old and poor; too poor to move from my village to the

---

[176] *Ibid.*

south. My cabins have been built with my own hands; my fields cultivated by only myself. I am attached to the spot improved by my own labor, and cannot believe that my friends will drive me from it.[177]

The U.S. commissioners at Moultrie Creek, Col. James Gadsden among them, called Neamathla their "friend and brother." After listening to his talk and remembering that even Andrew Jackson had recommended that he and a handful of other chiefs be left alone, they agreed to allow him to settle on a 2 square mile reservation along Rocky Comfort Creek in Gadsden County. The chief signed the treaty and accepted the grant of land, but never lived there. When he was offered money for his lands by the whites, who believed that he would move south to Central Florida, he accepted the money but instead relocated up the Chattahoochee River to what remained of the Creek Nation. He returned to Hitchiti, the town of his ancestors, and was an important chief there by the time of the 1833 Creek Census.[178]

The old chief raised the "red stick" one last time during the Creek War of 1836. He did not wish to be moved to a new home west of the Mississippi and fought alongside the Hitchiti, Yuchi and a few other outnumbered towns against the armies of Georgia, Alabama and the United States. Neamathla was captured and taken as a prisoner to Fort Mitchell where he was placed in chains. It is said that he never murmured a complaint, but stoically walked the Trail of Tears to Oklahoma that winter, a Creek warrior to the last.

---

[177] Talk of Neamathla during the negotiations of the Treaty of Moultrie Creek, delivered on September 11, 1823, *American State Papers – Indian Affairs*, Volume II: 437-438.
[178] Additional Article, Treaty of Moultrie Creek, 1823, *American State Papers – Indian Affairs*, Volume II: 430; Creek Census of 1833, Hitchiti Town, National Archives.

Photographs

Col. Benjamin Hawkins
Library of Congress

The Prophet Josiah Francis
National Museum of Great Britain

Tenskwatawa, the Shawnee Prophet

Neamathla (Eneah Emathla)

Fort Jackson in Wetumpka, Alabama

Moat of the "Negro Fort" at Prospect Bluff, Florida

William McIntosh

Timpoochee Barnard

Maj. Gen. Edmund P. Gaines

Lt. Col. Duncan L. Clinch

The forks of the Chattahoochee and Flint Rivers today

Restored blockhouse at Fort Gaines, Georgia

Site of Fort Scott in Decatur County, Georgia

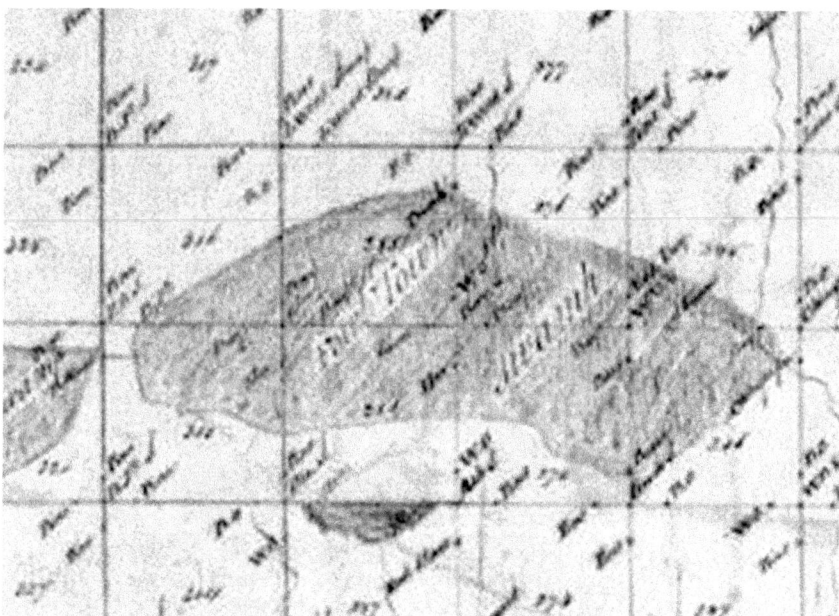

Fowltown Swamp as mapped in 1819

Four Mile Creek in Decatur County, Georgia

Fowltown marker in Decatur County, Georgia

Site of Fort Hughes in Bainbridge, Georgia

U.S. Government monument placed to mark grave of Aaron Hughes

Site of the Scott Massacre at Chattahoochee, Florida

Lake Miccosukee between Tallahassee and Monticello, Florida

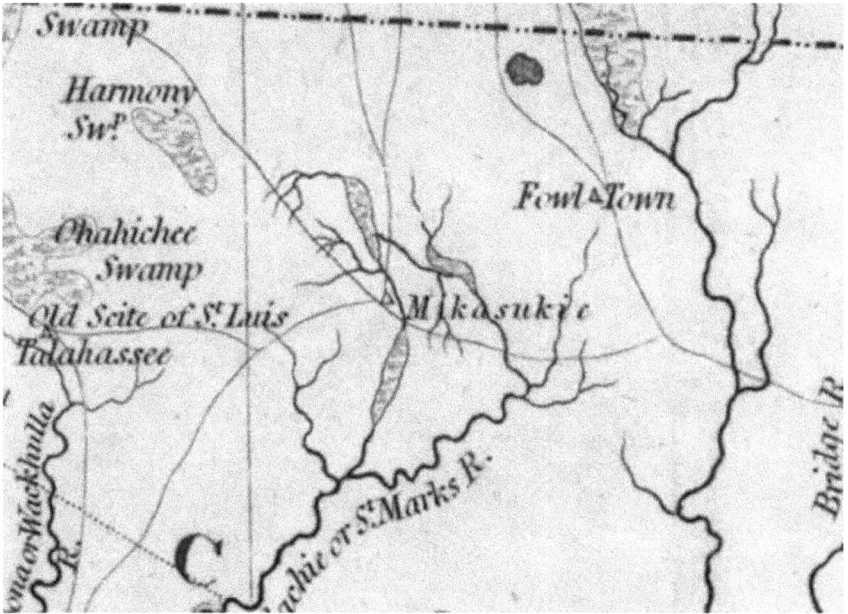

Historic map showing sites of Miccosukee and Fowltown in 1818

1Fort Gibson in Oklahoma, last stop on the Muscogee (Creek) Trail of Tears

References

Additional References

Books & Articles

Boyd, Mark F., "Historic Sites in and around the Jim Woodruff Reservoir," *River Basin Surveys Papers*, No. 13, Smithsonian Institute, Washington, D.C., 1958

Brantley, J.E., "A Report on the Limestones and Marls of the Coastal Plain of Georgia," *Bulletin No. 21*, Atlanta, Georgia.

Cashin, Edward J., *The King's Ranger: Thomas Brown and the American Revolution on the Southern Frontier*, University of Georgia Press, Athens, 1989.

Cox, Dale, *Nicolls' Outpost*, Old Kitchen Books, Bascom, Florida, 2015.

Cox, Dale, *The Scott Massacre of 1817*, West Gadsden Historical Society and Old Kitchen Books, Bascom, Florida, 2013.

Cox, Dale, *The Fort at Prospect Bluff*, Old Kitchen Books, Bascom, Florida, Scheduled for release during the winter of 2017-2018.

Cox, Dale and Rachael Conrad, *Fort Gaines, Georgia: A Military History*, Old Kitchen Books, Bascom, Florida, 2016

Din, Gilbert C., *War on the Gulf Coast: The Spanish Fight against William Augustus Bowles*, University Presses of Florida, Gainesville, 2012.

Hawkins, Benjamin, *Creek Confederacy and a Sketch of the Creek Country*, Savannah, Georgia, 1848.

Hawkins, Benjamin, *Letters of Benjamin Hawkins*, Savannah, Georgia,

Irving, Washington, *The Works of Washington Irving*, Author's Revist Edition, Volume XVI, "Woolfer5's Roost", G.P. Putnam, New York, 1863.

"Philo Pacificus," *Friend of Peace*, Volume II, Cambridge, 1821: 16.

Ridgeway, James (Ed.), *The Trials of A. Arbuthnot and R.C. Ambrister*, Published by James Ridgeway, London, 1819.

U.S. Government, *American State Papers* (Indian Affairs, Military Affairs & Foreign Affairs), Government Printing Office, Washington, D.C., various publication dates.

White, Nancy Marie, *et. al.*, "Archeology at Lake Seminole" Cleveland Museum of National History, Cleveland, Ohio, 1980.

Newspapers

Alexandria Gazette, October 24, 1817.

American Advocate, December 27, 1817.

American Telegraph, February 15, 1815.

Baltimore Patriot, May 5, 1816

Charleston City Gazette, November 20, 1817

Daily National Intelligencer, August 10, 1814

Georgia Journal, August 10, 1814; September 7, 1814; November 2, 9 & 23, 1814; May 6, 1817; June 24, 1817, December 2,1817;

The London Gazette, June 18, 1814

New York Commercial Advertiser, December 15, 1817.

New York Daily Advertiser, December 27, 1817.

Salem Gazette, May 21, 1816.

Savannah Republican, January 15, 1815.

The Times of London, August 13, 1818; August 15, 1818.

Index

169

www.ingramcontent.com/pod-product-compliance
Lightning Source LLC
Chambersburg PA
CBHW060050100426
42742CB00014B/2763